# THE RAWHIDE YEARS

Also by Glenn Vernam

*FICTION*

INDIAN HATER

PIONEER BREED

REDMAN IN WHITE MOCCASINS

THE TALKING RIFLE

*NON-FICTION*

MAN ON HORSEBACK

THEY SADDLED THE WEST

# GLENN R. VERNAM

# THE
# RAWHIDE
# YEARS

## *A History of the Cattlemen and the Cattle Country*

*Doubleday & Company, Inc., Garden City, New York, 1976*

Library of Congress Cataloging in Publication Data

Vernam, Glenn R
  The rawhide years,

  Bibliography: p. 221
  Includes index.
1. Cowboys—The West.   2. Frontier and pioneer life—The West.
3. The West—History.   I. Title.
F596.V47   978
ISBN: 0-385-11465-6
Library of Congress Catalog Card Number 75-40750

Dedicated to the American cowboy, who, more than the great industrialist, the englamored statesman, or the notable figures of the past, stands ever as the spirit of America in the eyes of the world.

# PREFACE

For untold centuries, civilization after civilization has risen to the epitome of glory, then vanished, leaving scarcely a trace. A myriad magnificent cities of brick and stone have flourished in their splendor around the globe, only to crumble, one by one, into the dust. Kings and emperors, who once ruled half the known world, have passed into the limbo of forgotten things. Times without end, barbarism has succeeded the finest of arts and sciences, eventually raising itself to the polished status of its predecessors, then, in turn, been trampled into oblivion under the crunching boots of other barbarians. Fabulous kingdoms have dissolved into the dim shadows of mythology; great industries have disappeared under the force of changing times; knowledge of superb arts and crafts lies buried with unrecorded artisans; patterns of living, work, warfare, and the conduct of man's varied affairs have passed through a multitude of changes. Even religion has altered itself countless times during its long journey through the labyrinth of superstition, idol worship, paganism, and the multitude of conflicting beliefs which have ever plagued humanity.

Only the stockman, among all of God's people, has remained constant in preserving his heritage against the forces of both man's and nature's vagaries. It is as though his knowledge and way of life had been designed as part of the Master's original plan, a plan which could be neither destroyed nor greatly improved upon. Despite a few superficial additions and alterations adapted to regional circumstances, the ways of the stockman are little changed from those of his ancient ancestor. While civilizations rose and fell, empires flourished and faded into oblivion, and human skills changed most aspects of the earth's surface, the stockman went his time-honored way, riding hand in hand with nature through the centuries. Proud of his heritage, independent of blandishments, and self-sufficient in his endeavors, his glance has always been one of pity as he looked down from the back of his horse upon the cannibalistic foibles of an ever unsure and unsatisfied multitude.

Today, as of yesterday and the day before, the stockman surveys the future with a calm and undisturbed detachment. No wars, famines, pestilence, or downfall of the mighty will seriously impair his unpretentious and unchanging life. Come what may, an apologetic world will always return to his inexhaustible storehouse built on the age-old foundation of the cowboy, the cowhorse, and the cow.

G.R.V.

# CONTENTS

# LIST OF ILLUSTRATIONS

*Chapter I*

## GREENER PASTURES

There is actually nothing particularly new about stockraising, the men who practice it, or the animals used for that purpose. Mounted nomads were grazing their semidomestic herds on the Kirgiz Steppe and Turkistan plains untold centuries before the dawn of recorded history rose out of the ancient East. Lot and Abraham were having range troubles long before Ur of the Chaldees crumbled to dust beneath ages of shifting sand dunes. Jacob had figured out a clever system of selective breeding, as a way of increasing his spotted herd at Laban's expense, when the known world was still a puny little territory bordering the Mediterranean Sea. By the beginning of the Christian era, all the freedom-loving nations of the Eastern world had adopted stockraising as a way of life. From Egypt to the Gobi Desert, mounted herdsmen drifted their privately owned bands of horses, cattle, and sheep between the high mountain meadows and warm coastal plains with the seasons. Early autumn saw the cutting, counting and sorting of herds that preceded the driving of desirable animals to market. Every spring ushered in the ritual of catching and branding the season's offspring with marks of ownership. Between times, younger horses were broken to the saddle, rangelands patrolled, marauding men and beasts slain or driven from chosen territories, and the annual festivals or religious gatherings attended with a gusto generated by months of harsh loneliness in the wastelands.

The beginning? Who knows? It was somewhere back in the dim

mists of antiquity, when primitive man first discovered the pleasure of mounted transport and a permanent food supply grazing within reach of his campfire. Burning the marks of personal ownership on the hides of animals was, we know, in common use before any known civilization was conceived. Roping from horseback is definitely recorded as having been an established art in Persia around 480 B.C.; only the desert stars could tell how much earlier it might have existed. And so it was with the myriad other practices which mark the stockman of the twentieth century A.D. as a direct descendant of the man who ranged his herds on the Mesopotamian plains in the twentieth century B.C.

All this has evolved and come into being under the hands of the mounted stockmen, those free-ranging, bold-eyed souls who claimed no master and paid homage to no overlords. Their world was the land of wide horizons and endless distances, where their herds might drift with the seasons and the stars chart tomorrow's course. Free as the winds that rippled the grass at their feet, each a king in his own right, they rode through a world of their own choosing with no one to say them nay. And always between their knees, in every waking hour, were the tough and durable horses bred up from the ancient wild steppes, animals first broken to man's bidding by unknown primitive hands. Down from the north they came to spread the gospel of the mounted man's superiority across the Iranian plains, northern Africa, and southern Europe. And with them came the vast herds of sheep and cattle which nourished the economy of all sparsely settled lands and elevated them to a status unknown by village dwellers and subservient agriculturists.

This was the breed, ever restless and ever seeking greener pastures, which flowed westward with the Moors to enter Spain. There, they met and assimilated themselves with the southern European herdsmen, likewise drifting westward on a similar quest. Both had been developing sturdier cattle and better horses at each stage of their seven-thousand-year journey. Both had visions of some as-yet undiscovered Utopia, where only the rim of the world bounded limitless leagues of unpeopled grazing lands.

When Columbus returned from his epic voyage of 1492, bringing tales of the great uncharted wilderness he had found lying in the sun on the far side of the world, the stockmen's nebulous dreams began to assume the form of reality. Even Columbus himself fell under the spell. When he sailed west again, in 1493, he took as cargo a small herd of cattle, along with ten mares and twenty-four stallions. He was firm in his conviction that he could establish a profitable retirement proposition in the New World, which would insure his old age against the eccentricities of crowned heads and unstable ships.

Though certain miscarriages of justice landed the old explorer in a form of retirement he had never anticipated, the colony he planted on Santo Domingo grew to seventeen towns during the next twenty years, with most of the population's economy based on stockraising. And he set an example that was hard to resist. Every ship leaving Spain for the New World during that period was viewed as a passport to the storied lands of virgin green pastures; every starry-eyed pilgrim rode westward on the two-headed dream of gold and a well-stocked estate.

Nor were they disappointed. The countless leagues of lush, unbroken lands were a paradise for grazing animals. Moreover, the current demands for their products were a delight to all budding ranchmen. With a whole new continent to explore and settle, horses to ride and beef to eat were of paramount importance. Most of this had to be supplied by the islands. Spain was far away, and transportation was necessarily slow and limited, fraught with all the vicissitudes of storms, calms, cramped quarters, and the faulty navigation of those days. It is doubtful if the Castilians ever could have made serious inroads on the American mainland had they been forced to depend on the mother country for all their needs.

As exploration and conquest was the order of the day, the local stockmen waxed and flourished beyond their wildest dreams. Island-raised horses were selling at around one thousand dollars each in 1519. The less-valuable cattle were still proportionately costly, whether for beef or founding new herds for the settlers.

But this did not deter the newcomers of means. Ambitious young men viewed ranching as a close second to scooping up the gold on the fabled mainland. With acreages at their disposal, most of them were sowing the seeds of four-footed harvests while waiting for a chance at the gold fields.

The Spanish Crown helped things along by establishing a royal farm on Santo Domingo in 1498, for the purpose of breeding the first-class mounts necessary for further development of the New World. Others, such as Esquivil's colony on Jamaica, Ponce de Leon's on Puerto Rico, and Velasquez's on Cuba, were all going concerns by 1500. Hernando Cortez was one of the many to make his initial bid for fortune by starting a ranch on Cuba shortly after 1500. His contemporary, Martin de Salazar, was doing likewise over on Puerto Rico at the same time. Many others were investing all the main islands with similar ventures. Most of them were enjoying marketable increases by 1513.

The horses these New World ranchers brought to the islands for propagating their herds were of the Arab and barb strains developed over centuries by desert horsemen. The majority of them had descended from more recent breeding in the province of Cordoba, said to have been inaugurated by the Arab caliphate of that territory, who crossed the native mares with four sires brought either from Yemen or Hejaz. The resulting product claimed the distinction of being regarded as the best saddle horses in existence at the time America was discovered.

Due to the difficulties of transportation, only the better grade of animals was brought to America. Shortages of feed and water, along with various afflictions, often further weeded out the less-sturdy members. Thus it was that the horses which reached America might be considered the pick of a choice breed. As such, they were a worthy contribution toward the repopulation of the horse's ancient home in the West.

And America reciprocated by welcoming the newcomers with a rich bounty that soon manifested itself in a phenomenal increase in their numbers. Within two decades, the islands found themselves virtually independent of Europe in their equine needs.

It was these island-raised horses which outfitted the exploring expeditions and colonization attempts on the mainland. They carried the *conquistadores* across the continent to the Pacific Ocean and stocked the embryonic ranches in all captured regions. Less than forty years after the first Spanish barb was swum ashore at Santo Domingo, these animals were claiming their birthright from North America to the Argentine pampas.

The cattle, which we always find closely associated with the stockman, followed a similar course. When the West Indian colonists saw how well the few head Columbus brought to Santo Domingo had adapted themselves to their new surroundings, they all joined hands in forwarding the movement. Equipped with a few head of breeding stock, the temperate climate of the Indies made any hopeful aspirant a flourishing stockman. By the early 1500s, increasing herds were supplying all the beef for home consumption. They also provided a profitable surplus for sale to ships reaching the Caribbean. Along with this, island stock was laying the foundations for new ranches in Florida, Mexico, and Central America.

These animals were chiefly of the fierce Andalusian breed. They were wild, tough cattle, predominantly black in color and carrying needle-sharp horns. Ranging at will over the islands, they became as salty as untamed beasts.

Gregorio de Villalobos took six of these Andalusian heifers and one bull from Santo Domingo to Vera Cruz in 1521. This was the launching of an epic in cattle raising which eventually encompassed the western half of North America.

Cortez sparked further expansion by establishing a ranch in the Oaxaca Valley of Mexico as soon as he finished bestowing Christianity on the natives who survived the initiation degrees. Many others were to soon follow his example, dotting the valleys of Mexico and Central America with their holdings. Many followed the same proceeding in South America. Pedro Mendenez Avillas became Florida's first cowman in 1565.

In Mexico, there were going ranches strung the length of both east and west coasts by 1540. Coronado was able to outfit himself with a full complement of native Mexican stock when he became the first American trail driver by herding five hundred cattle and sixteen hundred horses and mules from Culiacán, Mexico, to Zuni, Arizona, in that year. Luis de Carabajal set himself up in the ranch business at Cerralvo, just south of the Texas border, only fifteen years before Onate founded Santa Fe as a ranching center.

Meanwhile, back in the Caribbean Islands, where this great movement all started, the number of cattle was increasing by leaps and bounds. Many of them escaped from their owners to roam at will in the back country. They became as wild as deer and as formidable as African buffalo. In the course of time, some of the more enterprising spirits among the settlers began the business of hunting these wild, ownerless animals for their meat and hides for trading with visiting ships. As the cattle were free for the taking, it made a fairly profitable occupation for footloose adventurers.

It also offered a precarious living for certain individuals who preferred to remain far away from constituted authority. The island Spaniards of that period had the unpleasant habit of enslaving stranded or shipwrecked sailors of other nationalities. To avoid capture, many such unfortunates took to the brush instead of calling on the dons. As the only inhabitants of the unsettled sections were the uninhibited cattle hunters, outlaws, escaped slaves and unlucky seamen evading capture, their camps offered the kind of security common among brother fugitives. And there, over a short period, was born a nice little industry devoted to converting the Spanish cattle into a commodity desired by shipmasters more interested in bargains than in regulations.

The smokehouses used for curing the meat were called *boucans,* an Indian word appropriated from the natives who taught them the art. In the course of time, the men who used boucans for their unlawful industry became known as *boucaniers.* They were outlawed by the Spaniards and hunted down whenever possible.

But the boucaniers were a rugged fraternity. Their time in the wilds had generated a craftiness and half-savage deadliness that made them a match for the blundering military detachments. Too, their hideouts were hard to find and harder to surprise. Along with this, the fact that most of them preferred a quick death to rotting in captivity made their elimination a hopeless task.

By the early 1600s, many of them had acquired small boats in which they went out to meet passing ships, and even transported their beef products to the French and English ports of Tortuga and Jamaica. Being already outlawed and openly desirous of avenging their treatment by the Spaniards, it was only natural that the more vicious members of the brotherhood should begin banding together to prey on the enemy's cargo ships. The capture of seaworthy vessels allowed the boucaniers to recruit more men and go farther afield. Thus, it was only a short time until the Caribbean was infested with the freebooters who wrote one of the most lurid chapters in seafaring history.

Meanwhile, the English managed to corrupt the French name

of boucanier into "buccaneer," by which designation the piratical fraternity is still known. While the crimes of the Spanish main were perhaps no credit to the American ranching industry, there is no denying the rather licentious part they played in it.

It was, however, the more salutary business of finding broader horizons and greener grass that led legitimate stockmen to follow Cortez and Villalobos into wider fields. Grazing land was becoming crowded on the more circumscribed islands; growing governmental supervision prodded with thornlike aggravation at the sensitive souls of these independent spirits; untrammeled freedom dangled its seductive lure in the West.

In Mexico, these descendants of Asia's nomadic herdsmen found their golden dream. Here was an untouched continent awaiting their drifting herds. Before them was the unrestricted freedom of a world that was all their own. They threw away their cumbersome old war saddles in favor of a new design of their own creation and adopted a loose-fitting costume to replace the uncomfortable conquistador clothing. With the Spaniards' long-shanked, big-roweled spurs on their heels and long, braided-rawhide reatas in their hands, they became the first American cowboys with the first horses and the first domesticated cows, to roam the North American continent.

Thus it was that these three great pillars of the cowman's heritage, first forged in the flames of Spanish conquest, were brought across the sea to support a fabulous empire dedicated to bold men and grazing herds. Not since the days of the ancient Scythians had such a small segment of any race so forced its way into the foremost pages of a nation's history.

*Chapter II*

## THE VAQUERO

It is the Mexican *vaquero* whom we see as the first figure to enter the great pageant of the American cowcountry. Or it might be more accurate to say that he appeared as two separate, though closely related, individuals.

The first Mexican stockmen came from two different sections of Spain. One contingent settled on Mexico's east coast, while the other found the Pacific slope more to his liking. Being rather provincial by nature and well separated by distance, each of these colonies followed the common habit of most European immigrants by clinging to their own native customs and ingrained preferences. When they began moving north in search of wider freedoms, still barred from easy association with each other by Mexico's rugged interior, each took his own peculiarities with him.

So it was that those who worked up toward the northeast took their own distinctive outfits to the Rio Grande territory, beginning in 1583. Their heavier saddles, equipped with wide leather skirts nailed to the inside of the trees, were designed for the roughest usage in a harsh country. Thorn brush and cactus demanded much the same sort of protection for the sides of their horses as had the jousting and mounted warfare of knighthood days in Europe. Similar danger to the rider's legs had likewise induced the invention of heavy bullhide coverings for these members. Called *armas,* these were little more than a pair of dry hides hung over the fork of the saddle so that they might be pulled back over the legs when riding against thorny growth. With their fairly short-shanked spurs carrying medium-sized rowels, these men set the pattern that was to be followed by most of the later southwestern American cowboys.

In contrast, when the west-coast vaquero reached California in 1769, he was riding a lightweight, skirtless saddle built on an open tree. Like its eastern cousin, it used a single cinch mounted on Spanish rigging (suspended straight down from the front fork), but was made less substantial throughout. His spurs were of the big ten- to twelve-inch conquistador type, carrying four- to six-inch rowels. This western vaquero was inclined to be more of a dandy in dress, as well as an advocate of more gracious living. The latter was due in large part to the mild climate of the Pacific coast and comparative freedom from savage thorny growth. Also, the open rolling hills of southern California worked toward his becoming a confirmed dally-man in his roping; that is, he used a free rope with which he took a few turns around the saddle horn after making a catch. This was in direct contrast to the tie-man, who tied his rope hard and fast to the saddle before making a throw.

During the early days, however, both methods of roping avoided the use of the saddle horn as a snubbing post. The first vaquero saddles lacked much in strength and quality. Trees were often made of the light cactus wood, while locally made leather tended to be of poor quality. Ropers of that period commonly tied their ropes to the horse's tail, the cinch, or an extra surcingle that encircled both horse and saddle. It was not until the late 1700s that improved construction allowed the western vaquero to rely on saddle horns for holding his catch.

Roping from horseback is an ancient art that found its way into history with a group of warrior Persians connected with Xerxes's army in 480 B.C. It was flourishing among the wild Sarmatian tribes a couple of hundred years later, spreading out over the Russian steppes and Hungarian plains. Stockmen from Mongolia to Africa were roping from horseback all through the early days of the Christian era. The Romans used lariats in a form of gladiatorial combat. Asiatic barbarians and Moorish invaders introduced them into Europe, from whence the conquistadores brought

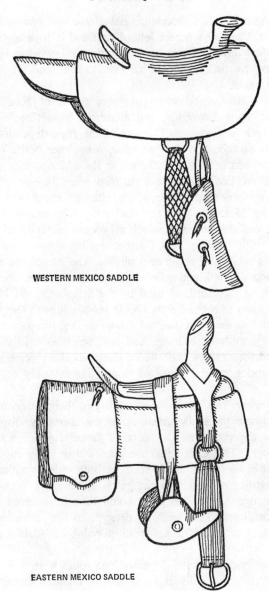

WESTERN MEXICO SADDLE

EASTERN MEXICO SADDLE

them to America. The succeeding *caballeros* and vaqueros picked up the art where the others left off, refined it to a high degree, added a few developments of their own, and produced some of the best rope artists the world has ever known, and probably will never see again.

Lariats used by the vaqueros were made of four to eight strands of braided rawhide, and measured from three-eighths to one-half inch in diameter. The size of the rope depended on the size of the strands and their number, sometimes both. The four-strand type was generally preferred, as the wider strands were less easily broken. Each strand was cut in one continuous string from the unblemished side of a cowhide after all the flanky portions and heavier backstrap were trimmed away. The strands were then stretched and soaked, after which they were carefully trimmed to uniform width and thickness. Further wetting allowed the braiding to be done while still damp and pliable. The completed rope was then stretched, oiled, and softened to an exact degree.

A lariat of this kind, as used by the Spaniards and Mexicans, commonly ran to around sixty feet in length, though lengths up to eighty-five feet were not unusual. There are records of some being up to one hundred feet long. And the men who used them were masters of the craft, a craft which demands the precise skill of a surgeon and a special sense of timing known only to sensitive hands.

Early visitors to California, in writing of their observations, invariably made particular mention of the dexterity displayed in roping by the vaqueros. One of their favorite sports was roping grizzly bears. This called for two men whose close coordination would settle loops on the bear from both sides simultaneously, thus preventing a dangerous charge on either rider. Stretched between the two horses, the beast could then be speared to death with lances, choked to death, or dragged to the ranch for one of the savage bear-and-bull fights so popular on California fiesta days.

In activities of this sort, the extra-long ropes were a decided advantage. Also, the dally style of roping made it easier for the rider to get loose from a dangerous victim in case something went wrong. This method was, moreover, easier on the rope. Rawhide ropes were all they had in the early days, and braided rawhide is susceptible to broken strands when subjected to sudden unyielding jerks. By taking a wrap or two around the saddle horn, a roper could allow the rope to slip enough so that any abrupt halting of a caught animal might be eased. This style of roping established itself all over most of the country west of the Rockies.

The Californio's roping was practically all conducted from horseback, as was the bulk of his other activities. He seldom did anything without a horse under him. And he was no less closely associated with his rope, using it with the facility of extended arms almost from infancy. Whether handling stock, snaring an animal for the ranch larder, hauling a *carreta* out of the mud, or overcoming some rival in a horseback duel, the lariat was always the first instrument brought into play. And its effectiveness in the vaquero's hands was seldom excelled by anything others might devise.

Some of their roping practices bordered on the miraculous. It was not considered unusual for a vaquero to dab his loop on anything within fifty or sixty feet or put it around any desired part of the animal. Practicing from early boyhood, they learned the secrets of the wide variety of methods necessary for the diversity of circumstances with which a roper might be faced.

There was the *mangana,* a forefooting throw in which a smallish loop was rolled out in a somewhat vertical position slightly ahead of the animal, timed so that the next reach of plunging forefeet would land in the loop. For the *mangana de cabre* (goat roping), a large loop was employed. It was thrown so that the loop twisted into a figure 8, the top part of which caught the animal's head while the forefeet went into the bottom of the 8. When the rope tightened, head and feet were drawn together to render the critter practically helpless. The *mangana de pial* was a similar figure 8 loop used for heel roping, each of the loops in the 8 taking a hind foot. In the *mangana de pie* (foot throw), the loop was laid out on the ground, with the hondo resting on the roper's toe. He simply pitched it with his foot when the desired animal was within reach.

These were only a few of the many special throws in common use. All met a ready acceptance throughout North America, though not all ropers attained the proficiency of the Mexican vaquero. Most of the horse-Indians gained a working knowledge of the art at an early date, passing it from tribe to tribe all the way from Mexico to Saskatchewan. All early western travelers wrote of Spanish-type roping throughout the Indian nations. Such records make it appear quite evident that roping traveled more or less hand-in-hand with the spread of horses.

When the early mountain-men began meeting the wild mustangs of the far West, they quickly adopted the Indian practice of roping such horses as they needed for use. They, along with the Mexicans, passed it on to the American stockmen, with whom it evolved into an everyday accomplishment in all forms of ranch work.

Something of a companion to roping was the old trick of tailing cow-brutes, as practiced by the vaqueros and early cowboys. The act consisted of riding up alongside a running critter and grabbing its tail for a quick twist around the saddle horn. Then, by spurring swiftly ahead and out at an angle, the animal could be flipped over on its back with surprising ease, providing the rider possessed the required deftness and timing. Such throws were commonly used to subdue chronic bunch-quitters or take the fight out of an ornery *cimarron* steer. The stunt was called *el coleo* by the Spaniards.

*El gallo,* another accomplishment which probably originated among the horsemen of antiquity, and reached America with the Spaniards, consisted of reaching down from the saddle while riding at full speed and plucking a rooster buried with only its head above ground. While this was used chiefly as a contest sport, mastery of the act would enable a cowboy to pick any desired object off the ground without dismounting.

Mexico in the sixteenth and seventeenth centuries was a wild and hostile land. Predatory animals ranged at will. No less savage were the native tribesmen who had not yet succumbed to the ministrations of Spanish benevolence. And after a few generations in the new wilderness, both horses and cattle absorbed all the untamed willfulness that was their natural heritage. Despite certain faults attributed to him by later Americans, there is no denying the courage, skill, and indomitability displayed by the vaquero during the two centuries it took to create and maintain his livestock empire, while ever extending its boundaries to the northernmost fringe of his country. Riding the half-wild mustangs or roping the still-wilder cattle, in a land where all the odds were against him, he stood among the leading figures in that great cavalcade of stockmen which had encircled half the earth.

From first to last, all his efforts had been of the most demanding kind. Nothing came easy. Most of his time was spent in skillet-and-blanket camps, where living was conducted in the most primitive style. Pleasures were few and far spaced. His cattle were the truculent Andalusian breed first brought to the Caribbean Islands. Most of them were descendants of the seven head Villalobos planted at Vera Cruz in 1521. Bearing stilettolike horns and tempers no less pointed, they had become wild as antelope and mean as wounded cougars. Time had served only to increase their toughness and restore their primitive hostility toward man. Yet their very ungovernable nature made them a natural for this raw and untamed land. And the vaquero could always figure ways to handle them. Aided by his trained cowhorse and equipped with rope and branding iron, he beat out new trails the length and breadth of Mexico. Careless and gay-hearted, he reckoned his grazing lands by the spread of the heavens and reasoned he could follow wherever a cow could go. From Panama to San Diego Mission and the banks of the Rio Grande, each season found him gathering bigger herds and seeking wider fields for his breeding stock.

Of equal importance to his spreading enterprise was the third pillar destined to support American cattledom. This was the Arab-barb horse the conquistadores had brought from Spain. These animals, first installed in the West Indies, had thrived and multiplied amazingly. Later importations had fused a mixture of similar strains with the original Cordoban blood to produce the typical western animal. Transplanted to the mainland, they moved northward toward their ancestral home on the Great Plains, gaining in numbers as they moved.

These horses were the lifeblood of the vaquero, as they had been to the conquistador. With them, he could go anywhere and do anything. Bred and trained to the mountains and deserts of

Mexico, no cow could elude them and no distance was too great for them to do the bidding of their masters. In the hands of the lighthearted vaqueros, they were the chief instruments necessary for whipping into shape that fabulous structure which was to exemplify the North American West for the next three hundred years.

*Chapter III*

## THE EQUINE TIDE

Though the cowboy and the cow stand as the most prominent supports of the cowcountry, neither could have risen to the heights they enjoy without the aid of that unique animal, the western mustang. It was the mustang which made possible the great roundups, open-range branding, and the leagues of riding necessary in maintaining control of free-roaming herds that knew naught of fences or distances. It was the mustang who escorted the great trail herds to market and brought their riders home again. Without them, much of the western wild lands would have long remained untenanted as progress fumbled its way forward on foot.

Moving northward from Mexico, well in advance of exploration and settlement, many became lost, or strayed or were stolen by the Indians. Some of the more individualistic animals no doubt turned their tails on enforced labor to take up residence on their own terms in regions far removed. Blessed with good climate, rich pasturage, and comparative freedom from predatory enemies, it was not long until sizable bands had reverted to the wild. Along with their propensity for drifting hither and yon in search of greener pasturage, a few generations found them advancing northward like a great rolling tide across the face of America.

Much of this progress was aided and abetted by the North American Indians. These people had as much affinity for the horse as the horse had for his ancestral home on the short-grass plains. Together, they created an impetus which engulfed the continent in little over a century.

It is believed that some of the horses taken by de Soto on his long pilgrimage through Georgia, Mississippi, and down into Texas, in 1539–43, may have strayed into the wilderness or been captured by the Indians. Perhaps something of that nature occurred among still-earlier explorers and Spanish colonists.

At any rate, La Salle found horses at the mouth of the Arkansas River, where he traded tomahawks for thirty-five head. This was during his exploration of the Mississippi River in 1682. He also heard of other animals of that kind on the lower Missouri River. Mendoza and Lopez saw horses in the possession of some Indians encountered between the Pecos and forks of the Colorado rivers, in Texas, the following year. La Salle's ill-fated landing on the Texas coast, in 1687, led him to a Caddo tribe, located near the junction of the Brazos and Navasota rivers, that owned some of the animals. Tonty had a like experience on Red River, near where Texarkana now stands, in 1690. As it would require considerable time for a few lost or stolen horses to build up their numbers enough so that they might be disseminated among the several tribes, it can only be concluded that these animals sprang from mounts brought to the gulf states by the early Spanish explorers.

Farther west, the sixteen hundred horses and mules brought to the Santa Fe country by Coronado in 1540 were the first ones to appear in that region. Castaneda, the chronicler of that expedition, gives us to understand that some of these animals were lost or stolen during their long journey through Texas, Oklahoma, and Kansas during the summer of 1541.

That either wild or stolen horses had advanced even farther north in certain sections before Coronado's time is a possibility borne out by some substantial bits of evidence. For one thing, the New Mexico Indians exhibited none of the awe and fear at sight of the strange beasts that had stricken all the natives farther south when horses first appeared. Instead, the Pueblo tribes showed an easy familiarity with the animals, being so eager to obtain some for themselves that Coronado was hard put to protect his herd from theft. Then there is the story of the horse used by do Campo, the Portuguese, in his escape from the Indians. This was also recorded by Castaneda.

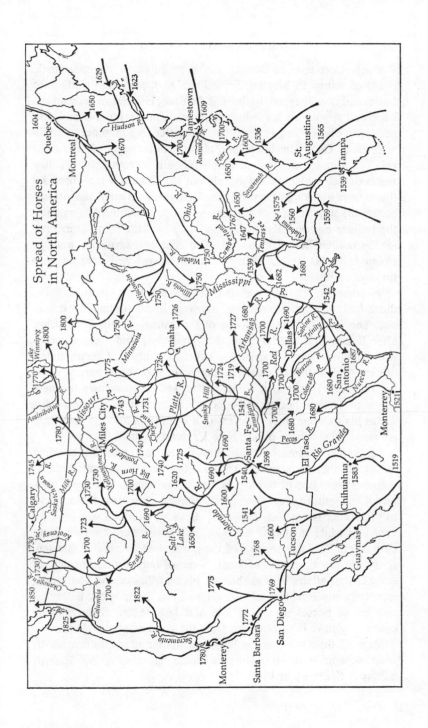

Spread of Horses
in North America

When Coronado, following his expedition to Kansas, made ready to return to Mexico, Friar Padilla, one of the priests with the expedition, begged to be left behind. His desire was to go back and spread his teaching among the Kansas Indians at Quivira, with whom they had visited the preceding summer. Padilla selected do Campo as his helper, along with a couple of lay brothers. The four set off on their lonely mission on foot. Though they reached their objective safely, all but do Campo were killed by the natives not long afterward. Do Campo apparently had no imperishable urge to uproot the sins of native worship. At any rate, the Indians allowed him to live and stay on with them. Sometime in 1544, thoughts of home impelled him to escape on a mare stolen from his hosts. Thus mounted, he reached Mexico City three years later.

Whether or not this was the only horse these particular Indians had, we have no way of knowing. In all probability it was not. The fact that they had one of the animals a full three years after horses first appeared in the Southwest, and were familiar with its value, would nourish the belief that they had accumulated others. Add to this Castaneda's statement that there were a number of horses lost, and it is not too farfetched to picture the new dawn of Indian horsemanship casting its first rays across the Texas plains some three quarters of a century before the first British steed came ashore on the New England coast.

All the early Spanish explorations in the Southwest led to some extent through Comanche territory. History tells us that the Comanches were one of the first bodies of Indians to develop a definite horse culture. Just how much relation these two factors had to each other is anybody's guess. This vast hinterland was seen by very few white men before 1600. Still fewer were the articulate chroniclers. Reliable records of the horse's early status in that territory are practically nonexistent. Some of our best authorities on early Indian affairs believe that the Plains tribes of the Southwest, especially the Pueblo and Navajo nations, did possess a limited number of horses in the middle and late 1500s. Such animals could only have been obtained from the conquistadores' herds.

Most of this, however, is largely a matter of conjecture as to what went on until after Juan de Onate had planted his Spanish colony at Santa Fe in 1598.

From then on, the picture becomes somewhat clearer. Onate was a fairly wealthy man from Guadalajara, Mexico, high in influential circles and married to a granddaughter of Cortez. His financial strength and influence among government officials was such as to make a success of this first permanent white settlement in what was to become the United States. True, a fort had already been built at St. Augustine, Florida, but it was scarcely more than a fortified garrison, having little in common with the building of homes, ranches, and business enterprises such as were to make Santa Fe a hub of empire.

Onate brought a large supply of breeding stock from Mexico to meet the needs of his 530 soldiers and settlers. The horses of both the soldiery and the civilians were the principal source of the equine hordes which later covered the West.

Onate's people hoped to keep their horses out of Indian hands. They were aware that mounted natives would be doubly hard to control. In consequence, some of the first regulations passed for the general welfare of the colonists were stringent laws forbidding the natives even to ride horses.

The enforcement of such laws, however, was another matter. Anyone as intelligent as the American Indian could easily see how the Great Spirit had sent such a gift to his people as an aid to hunting, going visiting, moving camp, and holding his own against the white invaders. His part in the affair was simply to figure ways of obtaining the animals without falling into the hands of the greedy and selfish iron-shirts. And his figuring was soon producing good results. Between tapping the wild herds and stealing the tame ones on raids through the Southwest and northern Mexico, he was soon as well mounted as the Spaniards. By the early 1600s, quantities of horses were spreading east across Texas and north on both sides of the continental divide.

By 1650, in all the great trading centers—where the various tribes met to trade Plains buffalo robes and beaded buckskins for Central America's feathers and California's seashells; beans and squash for pipestone pipes and obsidian arrow points; warbonnets and pad saddles for Spanish-made bits and bridles—horse trading had become one of the country's leading occupations. Members of many heretofore earthbound tribes returned home with seed stock that was to raise their status immeasurably.

Dawn of the eighteenth century found these western horses fanning out across the Texas plains to merge with those working west from the Mississippi Valley. In a long, rolling wave that presented a virtually unbroken front from the Mississippi River to the Colorado River of the West, they began inundating the Great Plains farther north.

The French exlorer Claude du Tisne found them in central Kansas in 1719. De Bourgmont located the northern fringe of advance up near the head of the Republican River five years later. By 1730, they had crossed Nebraska to the Dakota line. The year 1740 saw the tide washing up against the Black Hills. The plains of Alberta and Saskatchewan were next in line to be engulfed by the advancing horde, horses appearing there around 1745.

West of the continental divide, the wave rolled even more swiftly. Moving up the Colorado and Green rivers, the animals reached southern Idaho by about 1690. There, the tide split, one branch heading up into western Montana and the other swinging northwest to the Columbia River and British Columbia. Both regions found themselves in the horse business around 1730.

Much the same thing had transpired in the warm coastal valleys of California. Horses first came up from Mexico when Gaspar de Portola and Father Juanipero Serra set out for the north to establish a mission at San Diego, in 1769. During the next four years, Father Serra set up his first five California missions, which claimed a total of 200 horses and mules. Sixty years later, the missions had expanded to twenty-one, while their combined horse herds totalled 61,600 head. Along with this were the numerous *ranchos* which had sprung up between San Diego and Yerba Buena, all of which were well supplied with rapidly increasing horse herds.

The coastal natives were chiefly village-dwelling agriculturists and fishermen. They did little to promote the wave of northbound horses. Yet the animals themselves continued to flourish and spread, as they did everywhere else.

This movement was augmented by members of the Hudson's Bay fur brigades, which began visiting California shortly after 1800. Both company men and free trappers soon developed a marked preference for the Californios' Spanish horses. Trade, purchase, or gambler's luck often enabled these individuals to return north with the desirable animals. Later, gold seekers from the Oregon country were frequently of the same mind, acquiring a supply of the southern breed for the trip home. Enforced by both wild and Indian-owned horses, the long equine wave had lapped its way to the far northwest coast by the the mid-1800s.

Nor was this, in any section of the country, a mere niggardly scattering of the animals. The horse had returned to its ancient home, where he responded wholeheartedly. The luxurious sun-cured buffalo grass and gramma, the shoulder-high bunchgrass and bluestem welcomed the drifting herds with a lush bounty that few lands ever duplicated. With this were all the freedoms and untrammeled richness of life that is the heritage of all uncaged creatures. This combination of factors raised the American horse to the zenith of its power in the animal world.

By the time the fur traders, mountain-men, and a few hardy adventurers began probing into the vast wilderness beyond the Mississippi, in the late 1700s, they found horses everywhere. Wild, they ranged from Mexico to Saskatchewan; in Indian hands, they numbered from ten or a dozen to several thousand per man. The great tide had engulfed the continent.

*Chapter IV*

## THE COWBOY HERITAGE

The American cowboy seems to be something God created expressly for North America. No other land has ever succeeded in duplicating his completeness and his complexities. Daring as a cossack, yet courtly as a cavalier; steadfast as a dedicated knight, yet crafty as an Arab; tenacious as a Turk, yet carefree as a Gypsy; primitive as a hairy Goth, yet as aesthetic as a savant; gregarious as an Indian; yet retiring as a hermit; tempestuous as a Moor, yet gentle as a woman; courageous as a Tartar chieftain, yet bashful as a schoolboy; close-lipped as a Trappist monk, yet one of the wittiest and best storytellers in the world, he stands as the man who outfoxed Spain, Mexico, and England, outfought half a continent of Indians, outguessed the dictators of American development and built an empire to suit his own liking, with only the horse and the cow to aid him. And he accomplished the job with a speed and thoroughness that would have amazed every colonist since Moses, confused the bright minds of our eastern seaboard, and will always excite the envy of bumbling old Europe.

Indirectly, his ancestry extends back to the first man who ever straddled a horse. More to the point, he represents a curious blend of California caballero, Mexican vaquero, Rocky Mountain trapper, Dixieland planter, Plains Indian, and eastern cavalryman. Each of these added a different shade to his personality. Each bequeathed characteristics born only on western soil. Knitted together, they present the cowboy as a strictly North American creation possible nowhere else on the globe.

A large percentage of his basic qualities were inherited from the old-time mountain-men. Those hardy wilderness rovers represented the epitome of individualism, toughness, self-sufficiency, fierce independence, love of freedom, and bold daring. And they were a colorful lot in words, looks, and deeds. Many of their traits owed themselves to Indian origin. Others were a combination of red and white, improved in turn by each other.

These men must not be confused with the trappers of the East or the Canadian North. The latter were footmen and canoemen, following in the *coeur de bois* pattern. They were prone to maintain permanent headquarters, stuck more or less closely to familiar territories, and worked for the most part as *engagées* for the big fur companies.

Mountain-men were a different breed altogether. First and foremost, they were horsemen. Most were free-born Americans. The combination gave them an unrestrainable cockiness that was utterly foreign to other men of the wilderness. Add to this the immensity of the country in which they lived, the nomadic and survival talents copied from their native friends, and the urge to stand every man a king under his own hat, and we have the makings of a man that few lands have ever seen.

Washington Irving summed it up very nicely in his *Adventures of Captain Bonneville,* when he wrote: "A man who bestrides a horse must be essentially different from the man who cowers in a canoe. We find the Mountain-man, accordingly, hardy, lithe, vigorous and active—heedless of hardship, daring of danger, prodigal of the present and thoughtless of the future. . . . They move at will from place to place on horseback. The equestrian exercises, therefore, seem to make them physically and mentally a more lively and mercurial race than the unmounted fur trappers and traders, the self-vaunting Men of the North. Self-sufficient and game-spirited, one of these mountain-men is, with his horse and rifle, independent of the world, and he spurns all its restraints."

Other early writers have left us similar vivid descriptions of those bold venturers on horseback who prowled every hidden nook of the Rocky Mountain region before the rest of the nation ever got across the Mississippi River. They often spent months, or even years, in the wilderness without a glimpse of civilization. Horses were plentiful wherever they chose to roam. Game was more plentiful still. They had meat for their table and hides for their clothing; occasional traders supplied ammunition for their guns, Indian friends furnished human associations, and lithe, dusky maidens not infrequently provided them with warm tepees and all the comforts of home. With all that, they still retained their cherished independence and the right to pick their own trails. What more could a man ask? What society could give him more?

With only the stars to guide them and the lure of undiscovered beaver streams to lead them on, they might drift from the upper Missouri to southern California, or from Puget Sound to the lower Rio Grande in the course of a season. Hospitable as Indians, generous to a fault, and dependable as death, they could be as dangerous as cornered cougars, wild as the mustangs they rode, and as intemperate as any habitué of Nero's court. They recognized no master and obeyed no voice but their own. Nature was their god. They selected the colors of the sunset for decorating their shirts and moccasins; red and white earth painted their horses in the interest of display or camouflage; an eagle feather occasionally gave a knightly touch to battered wool hats. The sway of windswept grasses was in the long fringe of buckskin garments, which might also serve for the lashings and cordage that could not encumber meager packs. Blue was their roof and green their floor, while the Hereafter must surely lie just out of sight beyond the Great Shining Mountains.

Such a group bound for distant trapping grounds could have resembled nothing so much as an ancient Tartar horde sweeping over the rim of the world. Reinforced by a band of Indian friends, they might number a hundred or more men, women, and children. Included would be the wives and children of an indefinite number of the white men. All are mounted, herding along with them another two or three hundred packed and extra mustangs, which shuttle back and forth in a shifting, changing tapestry of black, white, red, brown, dun, roan, sorrel, pinto, bay, and chestnut designs. Beaded clothing, painted robes, and quilled tobacco pouches and rifle cases vie with twinkling trade mirrors, silver bracelets, and bright headbands as the kaleidoscope moves like a scintillating cloud across the open plain. Shoulder-length hair ripples in the wind to match the tossing of bead and buckskin fringes as a hundred supple bodies sway to the rhythm of spirited steeds in motion. The chattering of happy voices, the neighing of restless horses, shouted jokes, harmless threats hurled at a lagging animal. Perhaps there are a couple of French-Canadians to burst into sudden song, their brightly decorated *chapeaus*, long red sashes, and brilliantly beaded leggings adding an extra dash of color to the scene.

Level-eyed men with deadly long-barreled flint or percussion-cap rifles laid crosswise on saddle pommels lead the van. Indian scouts fan out on either side to locate game or a possible enemy ambush. Cherished Nez Percé horses appear here and there among the riders and in the horse herd. Youngsters race their spotted ponies with one another. Women drift casually back and forth to keep an eye on the security of travois loads and pack lashings, happy and proud in the knowledge that their men will be with them for another season.

Proudest and happiest of all were the women of the white men. They were ever quick to recognize the added wealth and attention lavished on their sex by the fair-skinned horsemen from the Land of the Rising Sun. The extra trinkets and gayer clothing bought for them by accepted suitors at some trading post set them apart as more fortunate and specially honored individuals.

Most mountain-men felt similarly fortunate in having such women as wives or companions. For, truth to tell, a large part of their success in the field was due to the feminine efforts in camp. The women skillfully and industriously cared for the furs and meat so toilsomely collected during the day; tanned the buckskins and made the clothing; erected and dismantled the tepees, saw to the proper transportation of belongings, and provided warm meals and comfortable firesides for homeless men destined to face the vicissitudes of nature and unpredictable red neighbors most of their waking hours.

North from Green River toward the land of the Blackfeet, or south into the mountain vastness claimed by the Utes; up the Platte and Powder from Fort Laramie; out from Bent's Fort with ever an eye for hostile Arapaho or Comanche. Day after day and week after week they rode through an empire that was theirs alone. Strung out like the wind-whipped tassels of a Frenchman's bright garters, or spread wide to resemble a curved section of rainbow tossed carelessly down on a green blanket, the assemblage rolled forward like a sun-shot cloud undulating across the dawn of creation.

On the other hand, one might take off for the Big Lonesome alone, or with only one or two companions, secure in the confidence that only such self-sufficient individuals can know. Six months? A year? Two years? Who knew? Or cared? Meanwhile, living temporarily with friendly Indians, pausing occasionally to smoke a pipe with some fellow wanderer, but mostly alone, their campfire ashes might dot a route that encompassed half the territory west of the Mississippi. Heedless of distance, weather, or hostile natives, a mountain rendezvous might lure him over a thousand miles of unmarked trails for a week of high revelry. Perhaps thoughts of a particularly desirable Indian girl would furnish an excuse for crossing the backbone of the Rockies for a spring hunt. Maybe the chance discovery of some unmapped beaver stream called for a journey that would have shocked conventional explorers unequipped for full-scale operations. In any case, they moved as horsemen have ever moved, tall in the saddle, eyes on the horizon, hearts lifting to the expanse of a new world designed to fit only the vision of giants and which only giants of vision could ever successfully claim as their own.

The great unsettled West provided a melting pot in which was blended the more practical features of Indian customs, horsemanship, frontier knowledge, Yankee ingenuity, vaquero skills, and the age-old indomitability of all horseback men. Here, the Latins' hospitality, vanity, hot blood, and a more polished adroitness in the saddle acted as a sort of leavening agent for the Northerners' aggressiveness and rugged individuality.

This was the combination which met a strong strain of southern-gentlemen and planter temperament moving west from the southeastern states to spread across the Texas plains.

The greater part of the migrants from the East were of the English and French cavalier type. Gentlemen bred of good families, and horsemen by training and tradition, they ever rode with the spirit of adventure and derring-do that has characterized the unfettered stockman of all lands in all ages. The western frontier, recently acquired from France, held an overpowering appeal to venturesome souls. Furs, gold, and stockraising possibilities flaunted their challenges to bold-eyed men who hungered for wider freedoms. It was a land for great visions. The majority of those who rode in pursuit of dreams claimed a background of horse-and-cattle breeding on homeland plantations. This led, in most cases, to a desire for wide acreages that would permit un-limited increase of livestock. In consequence, most southern eyes turned toward the south plains. And as an accompaniment, there came with them the inborn cavalier courtliness, spirit, and pride. Their militant temperament, egotism, and self-sufficiency comple-mented the Spanish boldness, ostentation, and faculty for reckless pleasures.

This admixture was soon augmented by new arrivals from Ten-nessee, Kentucky, and Missouri, plus a scattering of ex-cavalrymen who had found in the new West more scope for their imagination and talents. All were men of the long-rifle breed, tough and un-yielding, born to stand on their own feet and carve their own destinies on the face of a raw, new world.

Thus it was that the rugged individualism and cold, calculating blood of the Indian and north European met the expansive warmth, impetuosity, and lighthearted daring of southern France and Spain on the plains of Texas. There, the heritage that had ridden west with all the old world's horseback men met and fused into a single being that was as new as the untouched continent it faced.

As a matter of fact, it was primarily a case of the new meeting the new. This new breed of man suddenly found itself in a strange new world with an entirely new way of life to be developed. The whole land was a harsh and lonely place given to empty vistas and great distances. Nothing about it touched on familiar things. Thorn brush and cactus tore at their unprotected clothing. Open iron stirrups provided no shield for footwear too long away from home. Explosive mustangs demonstrated the inadequacy of flat, hornless saddles. Cattle and horses were as wild, and often as dangerous, as native beasts left to roam at will in a country as big as all outdoors. Only by the use of a lariat in experienced hands could any of them be captured and handled.

The newcomers had neither experience nor lariats; they knew nothing of the roping art. Moreover, the English-style saddles they brought with them from the East were practically worthless for such work. Had it not been for the Mexican vaquero and his knowledge of range life, the rise of the American cattleman would most likely have been a slower, and certainly rougher, story.

As it was, the budding Texan saw the value of emulating his Spanish neighbors and decided to grow up with the country. If building a herd of outlaw cattle from the back of an unpredictable mustang was the road to success, then he would fit himself to the best methods possible. The lore of his new vaquero acquaintances was all that was available, so he set aside his farm and plantation experience to seek instruction from this knowledgeable source.

He learned quickly and well. Mounted on a sturdy Mexican saddle, a wiry little mustang between his knees, protective bull-hide coverings over his trousers, and a rawhide rope in his hands, he was soon racing his mentors to the choice of unbranded wild cattle. Thus we find him in the late 1830s as a cowman in his own right.

And he continued using the dress and accouterments of the vaquero. Although, being a "Yankee," he was bound to work some improvements and innovations into the former's equipment, he still found it most suitable for the work he faced daily. Moreover, he discovered little excuse for changing any of the Mexican methods of roping, branding, ranging scattered herds, or breaking mustangs.

Even the heavy bridle bits and Spanish spurs, once accepted, were never relinquished for the lighter varieties common to the East. Such gear proved to be a necessity under prevailing conditions where, like the vaquero saddle, the need was all for distinctive western outfits. Too, from an aesthetic standpoint, the Southerner soon found that these articles were more in keeping with the old traditions of his cavalier ancestors. Spurs, in particular, were ever the badge of the true horseman. This medium-size, Spanish type from eastern Mexico was imposing enough to symbolize his status, while still being of a size for comfort and convenience when either afoot or mounted.

Wearing his spurs at all times was a confirmed habit of the

plainsman. A slightly modified form of the original Mexican design graced his boot heels through all the years to come.

Not so the old bullhide armas presented him by the vaquero. These apronlike hides, hung over the saddle fork, were both too unwieldy and inconvenient to suit the Texan's taste. He soon discarded them in favor of lacing up a pair of light-leather leggings which he fastened to a belt and wore like a pair of seatless trousers over his regular clothing. These provided serviceable and comfortable protection and would stay with him under all circumstances.

But he was still a vaquero, whether Mexican or American. The name stood alike for all those Southerners who worked with cattle. The word "cowboy" did not come into being on the south plains until about 1870.

Though the latter term was in use in Ireland around A.D. 1000, and crept into the English language before showing up in New England as a derogatory name for cattle thieves during Revolutionary War times, it did not appear in the American West until about 1835. Then it was applied only to soldiers detailed to rustle meat for the Texas army. For some time afterward, the word was fairly synonymous with "rustler." The "cowboy" designation, as we know it, apparently got its start in the Red River territory during the 1865–70 period. Some authorities think the "boy" part was brought to eastern Texas by settlers from the mountain regions of the Southeast, where "boy" was a common expression among the male element. Others contend that, as the majority of cowboys were in their youthful years, the "boy" appellation was used to set them apart from the cattle*men,* or ranch owners.

Out in California, the vaquero likewise remained in force throughout the range country. Like the men who went to Texas, the mixture of Indian, French-Canadian, north European, and American mountain-man, who drifted south to blend with the Spanish-Californian, found themselves in an unfamiliar world. Here, again, success hinged on the adoption of local practices. Cattle and horses were the country's economy, remaining for the vaqueros' skill to bring it to a profitable conclusion.

Most of the early newcomers, who found their way through the high passes of the Sierras and down into the coastal valleys, had long since learned that adaptability to existing conditions was the key to enjoying an agreeable life. The majority of them, already well experienced in the ways of the West, appreciated the worth of the early Santa Fe saddles which had assumed so much importance in the Rocky Mountain fur trade out of St. Louis. It was only natural for them to adopt the full complement of vaquero equipment and customs along with his saddle. In short, these men assimilated themselves with the Californios almost overnight, becoming one with the vaquero.

The scattering of American immigrants who came along later to settle under Mexican rule adopted the same practice. This was in the 1830 period. Foreign goods were hard to come by in Mexican lands anyway, so force of necessity helped them copy the native residents from the start. Time and continued association with local styles and ways soon led to full acceptance of all that went to make up the typical Californio.

At first, of course, this was more in the nature of setting aside old familiar things until fortune could remedy the matter. The American was inclined to cast a jaundiced eye on anything not of his own devising. Yet there was no denying the suitability of vaquero gear for current needs. Crude though they were, his saddles were quite comfortable, as well as most practical for everyday use. The later vaqueros had devised a *mochila,* or heavy leather covering, that fitted down over the open-seat, rawhide-covered tree to provide a better-fitting seat. This addition was held in place in a very substantial manner by having the horn and cantle thrust through holes cut in the covering to receive them.

Nothing better had yet been designed for riding the wild mustangs or handling the myriad phases of range work. The heavy wood-block stirrups, fitted with strong leather tapaderos, furnished excellent protection against thorny growth, cold rains, and falling horses. The big conquistador spurs, elaborate bridles, and highly embellished bits appealed to the flamboyant nature of those individualistic adventurers from the Indian lands.

One thing the American vaquero disliked was the old bullhide arma. He, like the Texan, found it to be awkward and cumbersome, and far from comfortable when pulled back over his legs.

Soon after his arrival, the American joined his ideas with the more refined tastes of upper-class caballeros to create something better suited to the open country of California.

The Americans had long been familiar with the neat buckskin leggins the Indians had devised a few hundred years previously. They found it a simple matter to rig a handy belt from which was suspended a pair of lightweight leather facings wide enough to protect the legs from occasional storms and the less-severe brush of that region. These leggins, or rather facings, were held in place by thongs tied around the backs of the legs. The Californios called this innovation *armitas,* or little armas.

Unfortunately, these facings often developed the bad habit of working around the leg out of position, while a broken tie string allowed them to flap in the breeze like a winged partridge. It

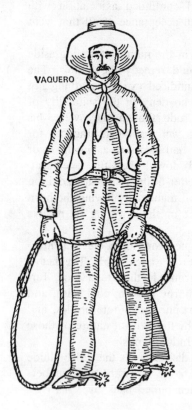

VAQUERO

BUCKAROO

was only a matter of time until disgruntled minds followed the Indian's more practical method of lacing up fully enclosed legs to make a substantial all-purpose garment. Called *chaparreras* by the Californios, American tongues soon shortened the name of this article to the later-familiar word "chaps."

It was also this hybrid vaquero who first came up with the idea of decorating the fronts of his chaps with the long, curly-haired skins of angora goats. Originally designed to add color to the caballero's showy outfits, these "woollies" later won much favor for their extra warmth in colder climates.

American influence was also responsible for the improvements in California saddles after the mid 1840s. The old charro rigs were lacking in strength for heavy roping. Too, the later vaqueros

PLAINSMAN

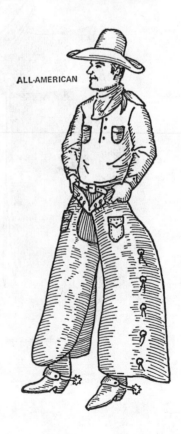

ALL-AMERICAN

found the short, stubby horn, with its saucer-sized top, somewhat less than ideal for the quick turns of a rope necessary in the roping practiced by the West Coast dally-man. They accordingly set about developing a stronger tree covered with better leather. The horn was slenderized, made taller, and shaped with a smaller, more desirable top.

At the same time, American dislike for the old Spanish rigging clamored for modification. The early mountain-men always liked the Indian method of using a centrally hung cinch. Transplanted cavalrymen and Eastern horsemen, who had always used single-cinch outfits, likewise favored a cinch that was set farther back

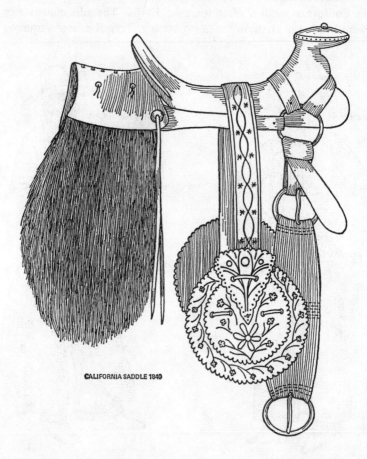

CALIFORNIA SADDLE 1840

than those used by the Spaniards. Their combined ideas resulted in the typical California saddle of 1860. This rig carried a high, dished cantle, the dally-man's tall, slender horn, the Californio's short, round skirts, and the American's centerfire rigging. Bentwood stirrups replaced the old carved-block type, making them more in keeping with the long tapaderos, carved leather, and silver mountings that are ever a delight to the western horseman.

After about 1860, this saddle remained the predominant type throughout California, eastward into Arizona and Nevada, and northward to the Columbia River Basin and Snake River region. The American usually fitted this new saddle with square skirts cut somewhat smaller than those used by the plainsmen. Such skirts were frequently rounded at the corners to eliminate the square shape's tendency to curl, as well as adding a more pleasing appearance. Otherwise, they differed little from the California style. They remained a favorite design throughout the intermountain Northwest until the Californio's short, round skirts were quite generally adopted around 1900.

Clad in the Californio's colorful trousers and short velvet jacket, big Spanish spurs dragging low on his heels, and crowned with a soft wool hat, the Americanized vaquero of the 1860s took his new outfit with him when he moved north into the Oregon country. There, he continued in much the same way. Only his name suffered a change. Corrupted by English tongues recently come to the Columbia River region, the Spanish word "vaquero" soon took its place throughout the Northwest as "buckaroo." And "buckaroo" he remained through all succeeding years.

By the same token, his trade became known as "buckarooing," while the contortions of the horses he often rode were called "bucking."

Basically, though, he was still the same old vaquero, rich in the traditions of California, Mexico, Spain, and the ancient East. And he differed only in superficialities from his counterpart on the plains of Texas. Today, as yesterday, wherever you find him or whatever you may call him, he is ever the American cowboy clad in the habiliments bestowed upon him by the vaquero and using the vaquero's tools, as he stands head-high under the ancestral banner of his illustrous clan.

*Chapter V*

## HOT IRONS

It is common knowledge that the branding of livestock is a very ancient practice. Man has used brands as a means of identifying his possessions among both thieves and honest neighbors for untold centuries. Ancient Egyptian inscriptions inform us that the branding of both slaves and cattle was practiced some two thousand years before Christ. An old tomb in Thebes has among its mural decorations the figure of a man branding a tied-down cow with a geometric design. The early Hungarians and the Mediterranean peoples spread the custom all over southern Europe. Records of branding in England have been traced back some twelve hundred years. The historian Jusserand says it was a common practice in Chaucer's time for men who kept horses for rent to have the animals "branded in a prominent manner, so that unscrupulous travelers should not be tempted to quit the road and appropriate the steeds."

The custom showed up in America about as soon as the first colonist got settled. Old records show that rules governing the use of brands and earmarks were among the first regulations adopted by the settlers. Perhaps the oldest one on record was at Plymouth, Massachusetts, dating back to 1636. History notes the other colonies as being not far behind.

The New Haven, Connecticut, Code of 1643 stipulated how branding should be done to prevent trouble among "the rightful owners of horses running in the woods." The Virginia *Gazette* carried a notice of strayed stock in 1751, in which was defined certain brands and earmarks. According to a record of December 25, 1734, we find the earmark that John Frie "Giveth his cattel and other Creatures is as following viz, a half cross cut out of the underside of the left ear split or cut out about the middle of the Top of the ear, called by some a figger seven."

We are also told by history that some of New England's more vocal advocates of Christian righteousness cried in loud voices for the burning of forehead brands on defenseless women upon whom God had personally delegated them to pass judgment.

None of this eastern branding, however, assumed much importance in the American livestock picture. Though it was practiced to some extent, particularly in certain mountain sections of the North and open pinelands of the South, the majority of the East saw little more than a moderate amount of earmarking.

It was beyond the Mississippi, among the free-ranging western stockmen, that brands and branding grew to full stature. And this came up the long trail from Mexico with the vaquero. It was the latter's inheritance from old Spain and the Moors, brought west by the conquistadores. Americans simply took up the practice in its entirety and went on from there.

Cortez is credited with having introduced branding into Mexico. That was in 1525, when he started branding his Three Christian Crosses on the rancho he had established in the Oaxaca Valley. This is supposed to have been the first herd brand in North America.

His neighbors, however, were not long in following his example. No doubt they already knew as much as he about it. At any rate, all the rancheros setting up in business in the New World were soon slapping artfully designed hot irons on everything they could catch. As the cattle industry moved northward through Mexico and into the United States, the selection of an individual brand for each outfit became an established practice.

And no better method of linking together free-ranging livestock and owners was ever devised. Nor since the days of knighthood has heraldic design so well represented a man, his family, his possessions, and the company under his charge. When America turned its attention toward ranching, it naturally accepted methods of procedure that two and a half centuries of use had proven most satisfactory for a new land.

As horses and cattle ran wild over unlimited territory from one year's end to another, ownership of young stock could be justly determined only by marking it with the mother's brand. This led to an annual gathering of all range animals in early summer, after the year's crop of colts and calves had been born and before they were weaned. With the unfenced ranges permitting everyone's stock to mingle freely, the owners soon discovered the desirability of joining forces to work the entire range at one time. The larger crew could thus accomplish the task more easily and quickly, as well as eliminate much duplication of effort, while allowing each man to supervise the branding of his own animals. Should he be unable to take part himself, one or more men from his outfit would be sent to join the crew as his representatives. Likewise, several small owners would occasionally go together and hire a single representative to handle the job for all of them during round-up. Such representatives were later called "reps," with typical American brevity. Their work was known as "repping" a herd or roundup.

History leaves little doubt that this sort of roundup in some similar form had followed the stockman all the way from the plains of ancient Turkistan. Although appearing under different names and with superficial variations necessary for different regions and periods of time, as it moved around the world, the American roundup was much the same old process of branding young stock, selecting the year's harvest of beef animals, and gathering marketable horses. The rodeos of the Mexicans and Californios were our first American version of this procedure, even though the Latins were somewhat prone to consider the range work rather secondary to the usual feasting, dancing, and horse racing.

The Americans approached the matter in a more serious manner when they got into the cow business. As a matter of fact, no owner who hoped to make a success could afford to do otherwise. Thus, at every roundup the primary interest was in seeing that everyone's stock was marked with the owner's individual brand. These letters, numbers, signs, or symbols might be traced on with the end of a bent rod, or a ring held in a pair of pliers or a cleft stick, but it had to be done if the man expected to claim the animals as his own. Later on, after rustlers and brand workers began infiltrating the range, laws were passed which obliged legal owners to mark their stock with stamp irons: i.e., branding irons with the whole design made in one piece. This type of iron was used on all animals in the herd. It would not show the variations common with running irons, nor would it accommodate itself to the alteration of any other brand.

Irons of this type even helped eliminate the old problem of maverick hunters, who had the unpleasant habit of stealing unweaned calves and running their brand on them after driving the creatures to some other locality. In most sections, the ranchers outlawed the branding of mavericks except during regular round-ups. There, they were either apportioned to the different owners or auctioned off for the benefit of the local cattlemen's association. After thus passing into legal ownership, they would be branded with the proper stamp irons. Such a procedure set them apart from any oddities that might have been marked with the less precise running iron.

Most people have come to know the meaning of the word "maverick" as applied to a stray or creature of indefinite affiliation. The name owes its origin to Colonel Maverick, a prominent figure in the early days of Texas.

There are several variations of the story about his name becoming associated with stray cattle, depending on who is telling it. The one perhaps nearest the truth has it that the colonel took over a large herd of cattle in payment of a debt. His interests and inclinations ran more to finance and business than to riding the brush after elusive longhorns. Then the war came along and help vanished. What with one thing and another, these maverick cattle virtually ran wild for a number of years, all the while increasing prodigiously. By the time circumstances again allowed the colonel to focus proper attention on his investment, the overgrown herd had flowed out over most of the surrounding country. Much of it, up to the four-year-olds, was still unbranded. These animals so outnumbered those of the less-affluent ranchers that the neighbors soon fell into the habit of calling anything a maverick that was lacking a brand. The handy designation eventually spread throughout the West.

Uninformed persons occasionally confuse "maverick" with "dogie," but this is a mistake. A dogie may easily become a maverick, if not discovered and properly branded, but it is first and foremost an orphaned calf left to its own resources. If branding saves it from becoming a maverick, it simply takes its place as a member of the herd in good standing.

Searing a brand on an animal's hide identifies it for all future time. It won't rub off or wear off, nor become lost or mislaid. Though stock may intermingle by the thousands over hundreds of miles of territory, or perhaps drift to parts unknown under stress of storm, drought, or plain cussedness, the brand is always there to denote its ownership. Strays found so far from home that the brand has never been heard of seldom represent a loss to the owner. Somewhere that mark belongs to a name and the name has an address. Both are on record with the state brand authorities. It is only a matter of time until cow and owner are brought together. Or, if the cow is marketed, in lieu of locating the man to whom she belongs, state brand inspectors forward the sales receipts for the animal to the name under which the brand is recorded. In case of change of ownership the original brand was *vented* by burning a line through it. This "erased" it and the new owner's brand was burned in the proper position on the critter. As a method of property management, it has few equals. No other business system has won so much respect for his effectiveness or been so well respected by its participants.

Unfortunately, the early days of American ranching saw branding employed as sort of a catch-as-catch-can proposition. Owners simply invented brands that apealed to their individual tastes, without too much thought about conflicting interests. This worked fairly well in the easygoing days of Spanish California and Texas, when ranches were few and civilized progress had not yet sown the seed of economic greed. But as the population grew and the number of owners increased, the inevitable duplication of brands began to appear. This led to the equally inevitable confusion, which, without authoritative supervision and controls, often ran into trouble.

Too, such conditions provided a fertile field for the ever-present scalawags who appear as if by magic in the wake of any expanding develoment. Haphazard branding offered a bonanza to such as they. A man could select a favorable territory, and then, taking for himself, let us say, the Bar 88 brand, be able to rebrand as his own the CC stock of his northern neighbor, any J6 animals belonging to the man to the south, the Bar 7U stuff from the eastern end of the valley, and Old Man Hewlitt's Bar H horses from over the mountain to the west. When clouds of suspicion began to hover uncomfortably close above his head, the miscreant could simply move to some distant location and start all over again.

It was chiefly to combat such undesirable practices that thoughtful minds began setting up registry systems in the various territories. By allowing the lawful use of only duly registered brands which did not conflict with or bear close resemblance to those already employed by residents of a given region, it became rather difficult for brand workers to ply their art undetected. This, coupled with the compulsory use of stamp irons, almost eradicated all ordinary range thievery.

Although various brands had been recorded with California authorities as early as 1786, it was not until changing conditions forced the issue that Governor Figueroa made it compulsory, in 1833, for all brand owners in the state to have their brands recorded and obtain a license for their use. One of the first of these to be so registered was that of Don Juan Avila.

Down in Texas, Stephen F. Austin had one of the first brands among the American settlers, acquired soon after his arrival in that state. It showed a strong reflection of the old Mexican pattern, as did most American brands in the Southwest at that time.

Brand recording in Texas, however, did not start until some time after Austin's advent on the scene. Some historians believe Richard H. Chisholm's HC Bar, registered March 4, 1832, to have been the first brand recorded in the state. Yet another good authority cites Eben Haven's Big E of 1831 as having that honor. In any event, Texas brands were synonymous with Texas ranches from the start.

New Mexico claims as its oldest brand the Cowhead. It is still owned by descendants of Cabeza de Vaca.

The Myers' M Hook is Wyoming's oldest brand to have been in continuous use by the same family since pioneer days.

Over in Oregon, we find Russell Dement's Big D holding the honor of being the first brand to be either used or registered in

# EARLY BRANDS

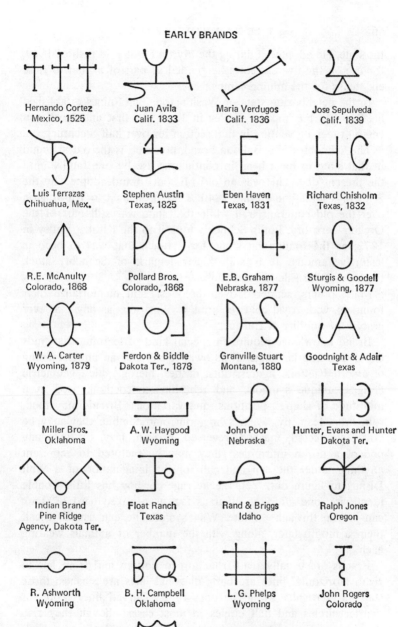

Hernando Cortez
Mexico, 1525

Juan Avila
Calif. 1833

Maria Verdugos
Calif. 1836

Jose Sepulveda
Calif. 1839

Luis Terrazas
Chihuahua, Mex.

Stephen Austin
Texas, 1825

Eben Haven
Texas, 1831

Richard Chisholm
Texas, 1832

R.E. McAnulty
Colorado, 1868

Pollard Bros.
Colorado, 1868

E.B. Graham
Nebraska, 1877

Sturgis & Goodell
Wyoming, 1877

W. A. Carter
Wyoming, 1879

Ferdon & Biddle
Dakota Ter., 1878

Granville Stuart
Montana, 1880

Goodnight & Adair
Texas

Miller Bros.
Oklahoma

A. W. Haygood
Wyoming

John Poor
Nebraska

Hunter, Evans and Hunter
Dakota Ter.

Indian Brand
Pine Ridge
Agency, Dakota Ter.

Float Ranch
Texas

Rand & Briggs
Idaho

Ralph Jones
Oregon

R. Ashworth
Wyoming

B. H. Campbell
Oklahoma

L. G. Phelps
Wyoming

John Rogers
Colorado

P. E. Melville
Washington

E. J. Reid
Nebraska

the state. He adopted it during the Myrtle Point gold rush of 1849, for use on the five elk cows he gentled as part of a plan to raise elk steaks for the mining camps.

In the neighboring state of Washington, Ben Snipes established his Big S in the Yakima Valley in 1855, the first and most successful ranching venture in that section for over half a century.

The Schneblys' Bar Balloon brand, however, is the oldest brand in that state to have been in continuous use by one family until the present day. This was an old Missouri brand adopted by the Schneblys sometime around 1840. They brought it to Washington over the old emigrant trail while that state was still part of the Oregon Territory. Philip Schnebly took it to the Kittitas Valley in 1872, as the foundation stone for a ranch that was to become lastingly famous. It is still the trademark of Schnebly stock throughout the Ellensburg region.

Many others, scattered over the West, still memorialize their founders, with royal coats of arms as illustrious as any that ever graced the nobility of Europe.

Brand knowledge requires a special kind of learning that finds expression in a language all its own. It calls for an understanding of assorted letters, figures, dots, dashes, hieroglyphics, geometric designs, unique symbols, and rebuslike concoctions used in a multitude of shapes, positions, and variations. Brands may rock, roll, drag, lean, fly, walk, swing, run, and tumble; they may be crazy, connected, mashed, reversed, broken, lazy, or have any one of a dozen infirmities; they may be pictured to represent anything under the sun and call for the imagination of a Walt Disney to figure out. Yet, the average cowboy has little trouble identifying one after the other as fast as a mixed herd of stock can be run through a chute. What's more, he can usually recall them a month later, along with the number of animals wearing each.

Brands are usually read from top to bottom and from left to right. Horizontal lines are bars; diagonal lines are slashes; those standing vertically would be ones or Is. Curved lines represent quarter circles and half circles in most cases, though they also serve as swings, rockers, and whatnot. Right angles become half boxes or rafters.

The translation of any group of two or more figures or letters

# BRAND LANGUAGE

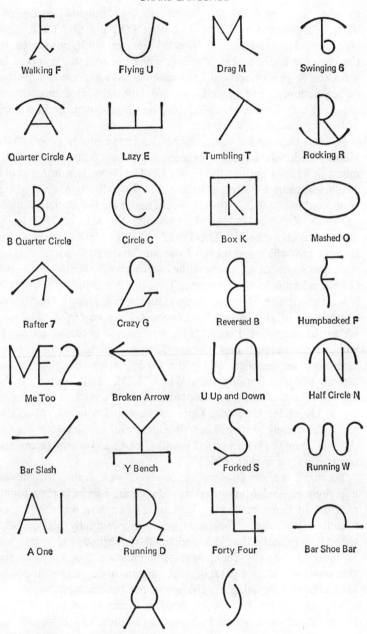

Walking **F**  
Flying **U**  
Drag **M**  
Swinging **6**

Quarter Circle **A**  
Lazy **E**  
Tumbling **T**  
Rocking **R**

**B** Quarter Circle  
Circle **C**  
Box **K**  
Mashed **O**

Rafter **7**  
Crazy **G**  
Reversed **B**  
Humpbacked **F**

Me Too  
Broken Arrow  
**U** Up and Down  
Half Circle **N**

Bar Slash  
**Y** Bench  
Forked **S**  
Running **W**

**A** One  
Running **D**  
Forty Four  
Bar Shoe Bar

Keyhole **A**  
Quien Sabe

together is often a single slurred word or fanciful expression. Thus, KTY would be Katy; B, Barby; OX, Big Ox; UBT, You Bet; S2N, Stewed Hen. An inverted quarter circle connected to the top of a figure makes it swing, while underneath, it serves as a rocker. A pair of vertical lines under it may represent a variety of leg actions, or if angled outward from the top, answer for wings. It may have a humped back, be up or down, be in a box, or be lazy enough to lie down.

It is not unusual for men, ranches, and even places to lose their identity under the names of brands. A cowboy riding for the 7UP might be known only as the Seven Up Kid. A certain horse could easily win rangewide recognition as the Lazy S Roan. Everything connected with the XX Ranch would make up the Double X outfit. Hank Kelley's HL brand earns him the title of Hell Kelly throughout the country. The Pitchfork spread gives its name to the new post office and much of the surrounding territory.

By the same token, personalities often reveal themselves in the brands selected by their owners. Tom Smith's simple TS displays his commonplace, down-to-earth nature, while Happy Jack Terry comes up with the Four Leaf Clover, adding an optimistic flourish to the stem end. Pete Coffin's wry humor enclosed his big P within coffin-shaped lines. George Sherwin had an eye for the future when he recorded S4 for the ranch he was building up for himself and three young sons. When H. M. Halff started ranching down on the pecos, he adopted a couple of vertical half circles as the brand for his stock. Upon being asked what he called the mark, he merely shrugged his shoulders and replied with a grin, "¿Quien sabe¿" (Who knows?) And Quien Sabe it was from then on to everyone in that section.

When all the amorous young cowboys were trying to win the affections of Old Man Plunkett's daughter, Lilybell, they found pleasure in honoring her by burning LIL on any mavericks they found on the range. The burnt offerings eventually accumulated to such a number that she registered the brand and went into business for herself. Then, ungrateful creature that she was, she climaxed the affair by taking an eastern dude as her husband instead of reciprocating toward any of her benefactors.

Various brands have been used to commemorate significant events, stand as signposts in business ventures, and represent im-

portant figures in western history. Burk Burnett adopted 6666 for
the ranch he won in a poker game with four sixes at Fort Worth.
No one could ever see the 101 brand without thinking of the
Miller Brothers' Wild West Show. Bill Strong's 47 totaled the
miles between his place and the nearest shipping point. Jack
Owens' Tepee was supposed to have been in honor of his faithful
Ute wife. The CN of Colonel William Cody and Major Frank
North was a living memento of the early West at North Platte,
Nebraska. Judge W. A. Carter's Bug brand marked the first entry
of range cattle into Wyoming's Big Horn Basin in 1879. The
Running W of the King Ranch in Texas spans a full century of
cowcountry development and is known wherever cattle graze.

An old Texas range classic is based on an ill-omened brand
that arose on the heels of a senseless murder. When a man by the
name of Poe quarreled with Fine Gilleland over the ownership of
a ten-dollar maverick, the affair wound up with a shooting in
which Poe was killed. This led to a range feud that cost the lives
of two or three more men.

Some cowboys had meanwhile expressed their distaste for the
whole deal by branding the steer with MURDER sprawled across its
side. By that time, no one would claim the disputed animal, give
it shelter, or have it in his herd. Even other cattle came to shun it
as a pariah or something unwholesome. The steer, accordingly,
was forced to range alone, a solitary testimonial to the indecency
of man, roaming endlessly over the face of the prairie until it
finally disappeared in some unknown fashion.

Another brand, carried for three years on a steer's hide,
cleared up the mystery of a slain cowboy over in Colorado. Jess
Hitson was the man's name. He disappeared one July day in
1868. No clue to his fate could be discovered. It was not until the
summer of 1871 that the mystery resolved itself in the appearance
of a stray longhorn steer.

The cowboys who came upon the unknown stray were first attracted by the oddly designed brand which covered almost one
entire side of the animal. Closer inspection revealed the following
inscription staring at them like a message from the dead: "7-4-68
INDIANS HOT AS HELL J H." The undoubted probability that Hitson had been about to brand this maverick when attacked by

Indians, and had managed to sear his message onto the critter before he was killed, left little question in his friends' minds.

No rangeman would find any fault with such reasoning. A cowboy's first thought is usually to slap a brand onto anything that comes under his hands. This may result in assorted deer, elk, antelope, bear, and coyotes showing up with somebody's brand on them. One Forest Service employee made some bailing-wire branding irons and playfully branded all the squirrels around his lonely station with his employer's well-known U S. Such pastimes often leave a record of activities that a cowboy's friends may read with all the celerity of an Indian scanning a painted buffalo robe.

He usually carves brands on his whittling sticks or the sandstone boulders beside his camping places; he burns them on his saddle, chaps, and other gear; he decorates the bunkhouse with brands, burns them on the furniture, and paints them on the canvas cover of the chuckwagon. He probably even scrawls them around the borders of letters to his sweetheart when he runs out of words. To all cowmen, they mean something, each unique in itself. And their meanings would fill a back-breaking volume. It would take another full set of books to hold the cowcamp sagas linked with untold numbers of them.

And with each brand there usually goes a set of earmarks. Ordinarily, the two are considered a unit, and so recorded. Certain arrangements of cut-out swallow forks, slashes, crops, underbits, overbits, jingle bobs, nicks, holes, and notches in the two ears not only help substantiate the hide markings found with them, but also serve as quick identification for the companion brand on casual inspection. Hide brands often become obscured by dirt, mud, manure, or the long hair of winter. It is often rather inconvenient to prod a bedded-down cow to her feet in order to reveal her brand, or read the brand on the off side of a moving critter. Earmarks, on the other hand, are invariably lifted high against the sky to face any inquiring observer. This makes for instant recognition even at considerable distances or under adverse circumstances. Too, only a rope and a knife are needed for a quick job of earmarking that will carry an erstwhile slick-ear dogie through the hazards of maverickdom while awaiting the annual branding roundup.

*Chapter VI*

## TRAIL DUST AND TALL GRASS

Southeast Texas was the fountainhead of the Great Plains cattle industry. The sturdy souls who first tapped its wealth had their work cut out for them. One fairly representative individual summed it up quite succinctly when, upon being asked about his success in the new territory, he said briefly, "I survived!" That so many of them managed to attain even this degree of accomplishment speaks volumes for their unfailing courage and resourcefulness. For it was a harsh and forbidding land. Thrust like a great bulky thumb into the western wilderness, and separated by great distances from all the gentler influences of eastern civilization it was a place where only men of iron nerve and wide vision could win a spot in the sun. Markets were far away and manufactured goods were practically nonexistent; Indian raids were frequent and living conditions most primitive. Cattle and grass were the only things in sight on which the new Texan could build a future. And the first and most important thing was to get the cattle.

There were cattle in Texas. They had been there since Mexican ranching first started, around 1665. In fact, certain Texas historians claim that some of the animals were brought across the Rio Grande in 1583, when Luis de Carabajal was establishing his ranch near Cerralvo, just across the river. Others were brought to San Francisco Mission, on the upper Neches River, by Capitan Alonzo de Leon, in 1690. What with the increase from old herds and new, as settlement developed, there was no dearth of the animals when the Americans appeared on the scene. The big trouble was to get control of them.

Many an outlaw-natured bovine, scenting the sweet winds of freedom in the unsettled wilderness, had promptly reverted to the wild. Unbranded and unclaimed, they ranged the brush country with all the elusiveness of deer and the savagery of a rump-shot grizzly bear. One and all, they took to the brush as had their un-domesticated ancestors, in many cases coming out to feed only at night. It was impossible to drive them out of the thorn thickets and into the open. It usually remained for their prospective own-ers to run them down and rope them, after which they might be tied to tame oxen and herded to the ranch.

Most of this roping had to be done amid the dense brush, where the cattle liked to hide in daylight hours. In the narrow lanes winding between the trees, where limbs hung low and thorny entanglements abounded, long throws were usually impossible. Wide loops were even worse. Being less adept at the newly ac-quired art of handling ropes, the Americans cut the vaqueros' reatas down to twenty or thirty feet and learned to make their catches with small loops that would pass through openings scarcely wider than the critter's horns.

Also, in view of the difficulties involved in even getting a rope on the victim, as well as wanting to make sure of staying with any successful catch, they discarded the old vaquero custom of taking dallys around the saddle horn in favor of tying the rope solidly to that member before starting operations. The latter style had certain disadvantages, but it seldom failed in keeping horse and cow together until a more-or-less satisfactory result was ob-tained.

As soon as manila ropes became readily available, most Texans discarded the old rawhide variety. There was less danger of broken strands in the fiber type when subjected to the sudden jolt of a critter hitting the end of a rope tied hard and fast. The manila rope also stood up better under the wet weather which often engulfed the Texas coast. And over all was the average Texan's antipathy toward conventional Mexican customs. They might adopt his skills, knowledge, and equipment, but they usu-ally sought to hide its identity under names or alterations which gave it the stamp of their own. The coming of the manila rope gave them a good chance to graft a Texan replica onto the old Mexican principle and have an object that revealed no foreign entanglements.

But over and above all, the Texan learned his new trade quickly and well. Working under the most adverse conditions, he was soon displaying in his rope work all the skill and adroitness that marked the performances of his Latin instructors. Succeeding years saw him developing original innovations and alterations in the craft, better fitting it to his assorted needs.

A throw of this type was the method introduced by John Blocker, one of the finest ropers Texas ever produced. Though most modern cowboys are familiar with the overlarge Blocker loop, which is thrown over a critter's shoulders to catch both forelegs from the opposite side, the identity of its inventor has become lost to many of them.

Another throw, supposed to have been invented in California, claimed some popularity on the northern ranges. Unsuited for horseback work, it was used mainly for ground roping. The loop was swung counterclockwise once around the left side of the roper, then brought across and back under the right arm, continuing up over the right shoulder, from whence it was pitched at the intended victim. Executed with a single swift, fluid movement, it was very effective where momentum was needed without resorting to swinging the loop overhead.

Other distinctive throws, too numerous to mention, were developed for special purposes under a wide variety of conditions. Backhand loops, vertical loops, and loops that snaked out low to the ground before jumping up to snare running feet were commonplace with most cowboys. So were half-hitches thrown around a post or flying legs to halt a caught animal. But whatever type of throw the roper may use, it was the basic sleight-of-hand taught by the Mexican vaquero that developed the cowboy of the Southwest into a performer who stands supreme in the craft to this day.

This is not to say that the rest of the West is lacking in its quota of top-hands in this work. They appear everywhere in cattleland, experts that any country might be proud to claim. But the plains and open grasslands of other parts of North America seldom imposed on a roper the demands that prevailed as every-day work in most of the Southwest. Taken as a whole, cowboys from this latter region have always rated higher in roping than those from other sections, due solely to the proficiency necessity forced upon them. This is borne out by rodeo records hung up during the past three quarters of a century.

But this professional efficiency is only a small part of it. It is in the everyday work on the range that the average cowboy's rope displays its true worth. Today, as yesterday, it is the paramount tool of his trade. Everything is done with it, from snaking an old mossy-horn out of the brush to dragging in wood for the cook's fire. He habitually puts a rope on anything he wants to stop, hold, or move, in duty or in pastime. Its everyday use makes it as much a part of himself as does the writer's pen, the soldier's rifle, or the preacher's Bible.

Uncle Dave Cummings of Buffalo, Wyoming, tells of a cowboy he once saw rope a prairie dog. José Romero of Tucson, Arizona, roped an eagle he found feeding on a carcass in 1939. Bill Davis of New Mexico got his rope over the neck and under one wing of a wild turkey. Johnny Green roped a Colorado schoolmarm's bag of books and papers out of the river, when her horse stumbled on a rock in deep water on the way home from school. Johnny's friends claimed it was only a practice throw, at that, a little pre-liminary to the main job of leading her up to the altar the follow-ing spring.

But to get back to the early days of the Texan who managed to survive. The survival depended solely on his success with the animals he had collected. Bulwarked by the vaqueros' skills and the heritage bequeathed by six thousand years of mounted stock-men, he eventually found himself riding into what seemed to be the fulfillment of his dream. Primitive though his mode of living and hard the life he was forced to lead, his horses and cattle now ranged on a thousand hills, while only the distant horizon marked the boundaries of his domain.

The rich, grassy lands of the new home generated in the Span-ish cattle an increase which equaled that of the spreading mus-tangs. The settlement of the Texas dispute with Mexico fostered the growing number of new ranchers throughout the southeast part of the state. Father Kino, who in 1687 had brought a herd to his Mission Dolores, in northern Sonora, had furthered the movement by taking their progeny up into the Tucson, Arizona, territory shortly after 1700. Onate's colony, at Santa Fe, had expanded into wide-spreading ranching throughout northern New Mexico, most of it based on stock brought north in 1598. Antonio Vallejos shoved on even farther north, to establish his headquarters near the present Walsenburg, Colorado, in 1847. Cattledom had come into its own the length and breadth of the Southwest.

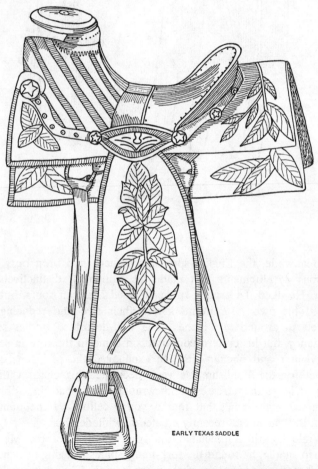

EARLY TEXAS SADDLE

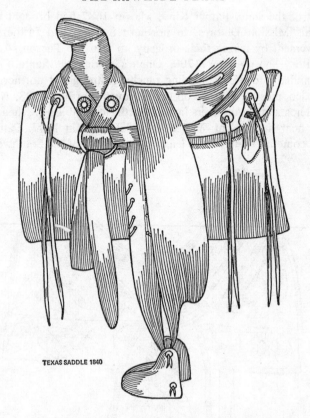

TEXAS SADDLE 1840

Meanwhile, the English-speaking vaquero had been busy with various developments that made his equipment distinctively his own. He liked the ornate, spoke-roweled Mexican spurs, but followed his own taste in modifying their size and reducing the rowels to around two inches. The well-decorated bridles suited his fancy, but his eastern conservatism came to the fore in selecting lighter and plainer bits. He exchanged the Mexican's short jacket for the Englishman's vest, decorated his chaps with Indian-style leather fringes, and wrapped his head in a broad-brimmed plainsman's hat that a young fellow by the name of John B. Stetson had recently created in Philadelphia.

While he still appreciated the good qualities of the Mexican charro saddle, he found the fork-hung Spanish rigging not entirely satisfactory for his style of tie-down roping. The unsecured rear of the saddle was inclined to punish both himself and the horse when coupled to a fighting steer a half larger than both of them. First, he tried anchoring the saddle down by running a diagonal strap from the cinch ring to the back of the tree. This helped, but not enough to suit him. He wound up by devising the entirely new idea of installing a separate, though very similar, back rigging strap that went over the rear of the tree to hang straight down and carry a second cinch. With the two cinches connected by straps at the rigging rings, and joined at their centers by a short connection, he had his saddle tied down hard and fast against any of the difficulties that had previously been a hardship. Then

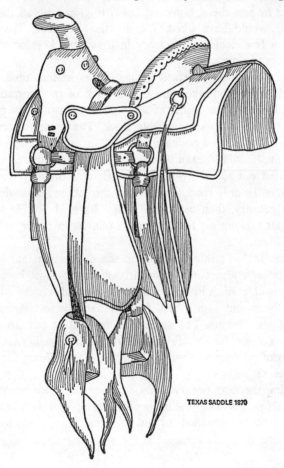

TEXAS SADDLE 1870

he transferred the Mexicans' inside skirts to the outside of the tree and lined the inner surfaces of the bars with sheepskin. He also discarded the old wood-block stirrups in favor of the bent-wood type, which had come into being in 1790, but retained a modified form of the vaquero tapaderos.

First developed around 1850, this was the forerunner of the popular double rigged saddle which was to signify the plains cowboy for over three quarters of a century.

Thus equipped for a destiny that was to eventually exceed his wildest visions, the Texan surveyed his growing herds and began speculating on a glowing future.

What he saw there, however, failed to glow with all the brightness he would have liked. Despite their number, Texas cattle lacked a few elements necessary in a suitable key for unlocking the doors of prosperity.

The most serious obstacle facing Texas at that time was the great distance to market and a total lack of transportation. The few hide-and-tallow works at some of the gulf ports were practically the only outlets for salable stock. The scanty returns to be obtained from such a poor market were far from encouraging.

But the budding Texan was as tough as his environment. When he started out to do a job, he aimed to finish it. If cattle and grass was the only road to success in the jobless, moneyless, marketless country, then cattle and grass it would be. He therefore set about racking his fertile Texas brain for a better solution to his problem.

It was in 1842 that he came to the conclusion that his long-legged steers, who could outwalk and outrun most horses, were quite capable of walking to a more profitable destination. He promptly set out with a herd for New Orleans to test the soundness of his thinking. The success of the venture put store-bought clothes on his family and transformed the longhorn cow into the star of promise that was to light the state of Texas for decades to come.

During the next twenty years, an increasing number of clacking hoofs pounded out the design for an empire over half a nation. Other herds were trailed to New Orleans. Many went to Shreveport for boat shipment to the gulf markets. At least one herd was swum across the Mississippi River, below the mouth of the Red, en route to Woodville, Mississippi. Edward Piper drove 1,000 head to Ohio in 1846. Several went to the California gold fields in 1849–50. Pointing and Malone trailed 680 head of 1,200-pound steers to Muncie, Indiana, in 1852, from whence they were shipped to New York by rail. Oliver Loving reached Illinois with a herd in 1855, and Chicago got its first Texas beef the following year. The West had discovered its great heritage while the East slowly awoke to the possibilities of a new industry based on an unprecedented flow of raw wealth from across the Mississippi.

Here it was that the American cowboy came into being as a distinct individual. Self-trained in the ways of wild mustangs and wilder cattle, he learned to shield his body against the vagaries of nature and arm himself against the villainy of man and beast; to look into the future with unblinking eyes and stand on his own two feet before the world. His inquisitive mind solved the problems of better range breeding and trail driving. His skillful hands devised finer tools for his craft. His sturdiness against all odds opened a treasure chest that would have been the envy of every gold-hungry conquistador who ever sailed west.

Needless to say, his future was not all pie in the sky. Texas had not yet relinquished her overflowing bag of hardships. The long drives concealed many perils, while financial returns were ever in doubt. Indians and rustlers took their toll, as did droughts and freezing northers. The cowboy's home was usually small and mean; his clothing and equipment were often made of whatever materials he could scrape together; beef and beans offered scant niceties in culinary displays. Yet his dominant will kept him afloat. He felt he was surely paving the way to realization of his ambition.

It was at this juncture that Fate took another slap at the Texan. Aided by the pillars of refined society in the civilized East, the rabid abolitionists and the fanatic secessionists, it suddenly toppled the western empire toward the brink of ruin.

And it was virtual ruin that faced him when he returned from the conflict between the states. Tumbleweeds rolled across his untended fields while buzzards roosted on the sagging buildings.

Rags hid the knobby joints of his family when they sat down to a meal of greens and grits or gathered to speculate on the state of livestock scattered to the four winds. He was penniless in a state that was bankrupt. Former cattle markets had been crushed beneath the collapse of the South. Carpetbaggers held the reins of authority. The future was a dark void indeed.

But the Texan was still the same tough old warrior. His grass was still there, and the cattle should be somewhere around. He still figured a fighting man should stay on his feet till the roof fell in. Without any ado, he started righting his disrupted world the best he could.

Due to the federal blockade of the Mississippi Valley, sealing off the southern markets, plus the shortage of men at home during the war years, most of the country's cattle had been allowed to run wild, unbranded and untended, multiplying as only a kindly nature could contrive. They ranged everywhere. Big three- to five-year-old steers roamed the thickets, sleek and fat on mesquite beans and ready for market. Often ownerless and chiefly unclaimable, their owners long absent or dead on distant battlefields, cattle of all ages awaited anyone who would take charge of them.

There were an estimated six million head in the state in 1866.

Men with vision, courage, and a long rope literally took the bull by the horns during this period. With only hope and belief as aids, they gathered what identifiable stock they could find, and then added to it by branding as many ownerless critters as they could rope out of the brush. Many individuals worked themselves into ownership of sizable herds when they couldn't find six bits to buy a pair of pants.

Their original trouble was still there—no markets. Several ranchers drove small herds to Mexico, where they could be traded for foodstuffs, clothing, and the like, but there was little future in such proceedings.

A few herds were trailed to Arkansas and Missouri, but with indifferent results. Harvey Ray and George Duffield took a bunch to Iowa in 1866, meeting much trouble on the way. Several others tried driving over the old Shawnee Trail to the railroad at Sedalia, Missouri, but they were so beset by farmers and jayhawkers in the Baxter Springs section of Kansas that they gave up this outlet after 1866. Nelson Story took six hundred head over the Bozeman Trail to Virginia City, Montana, that year. He found success and a good profit, but the Wyoming Sioux were on the warpath at that time and most men figured they lacked Story's brand of luck.

Then, in 1867, the tide suddenly took a turn for the better. The railroad came to Abilene, Kansas, that year, bringing with it a visionary genius by the name of Joseph McCoy. McCoy's eyes were set far enough apart that he was able to view the prospective market for beef in the East in conjunction with the vast herds of cattle in the West. He promptly set himself up as a stock buyer. His first move was to hire Jesse Chisholm, an old half-breed Indian trader, to mark out a trail from the new railroad town of Abilene directly south to the Texas border, at Choke Bluff Crossing of the Red River. Meanwhile, McCoy had sent word to Texas by every southbound traveler that this new trail was the direct avenue over which three- to five-dollar steers could be driven to an eighteen- to twenty-five-dollar market, ready to absorb all they cared to bring.

Texas responded with an alacrity that amazed everybody, even McCoy. Thirty-five thousand longhorns reached Abilene that year. The figure was to reach six hundred thousand in 1871. And this unprecedented movement served to focus the eyes of the world on the new western empire built on beef, cowhorses, and the American cowboy.

And this was only a small part of it. As the railroad pushed on west, Newton, Wichita, and Ellsworth became buying-and-shipping points for the southern stock. Each new railroad town flourished under the rapidly burgeoning cattle trade. Along with this, uncounted thousands went on north to stock new ranches from the Platte to Milk River and from Idaho to the Dakotas.

About 1873, two events coincided to shift this great movement on farther west from the Chisholm Trail. Rapidly expanding settlements of Kansas farmers got up in arms about herd damage to their crops and the danger of Texas fever brought north by passing stock to contaminate their domestic animals. About this time, the advancing railroad had pushed on west to give birth to Dodge City. Dodge was a wide-open town in a still-wide-open country. The harassed cowmen, therefore, broke out a new trail

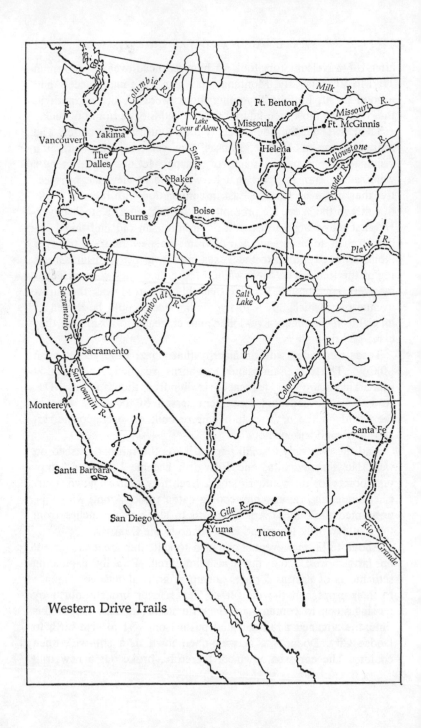

Western Drive Trails

from Doan's Store on Red River to the new shipping point. This Western Trail, as it was called, was to be the route of all north-bound herds for the remaining twenty years of trail driving.

Meanwhile, several individuals had discovered that the rich grasses of the north plains not only provided more luxuriant sum-mer feed than those of the South, but when sun-cured and dried down on the stem, would carry stock through the winter as well as if they had been barn-fed.

It was back in 1829 that a venturesome Canadian Frenchman by the name of Alexis Bailly trailed a herd of cattle from Prairie du Chien, at the mouth of the Wisconsin River, to the Selkirk col-ony at Pembina, North Dakota. Bailly's success with the little herd proved the worth of the north plains as a cattle country, al-though the experiment was largely lost sight of in the subsequent failure of the colony.

And there the matter rested for over twenty years. It was a man by the name of Seth E. Ward, a Fort Laramie freighter, who is usually accredited with being the first to attract national at-tention to the possibilities of year-round ranching in that region. Some unusually early storms the fall of 1852 prevented Ward from driving his oxen back to the Missouri River for wintering. His only recourse was to turn them out in the Laramie Valley, hoping some might survive to be reconditioned the following summer. But when spring came, he was happily surprised to find all his animals in even better shape than they had been the preceding fall.

Several other freighters and army men, overtaken by winter on the high plains, had similar experiences during the following ten years. By the time the Indians were crowded out of that region enough to permit any sort of settlement, white men had conceived a whole new image of western ranching. All they needed was cattle.

Texas had the cattle. Texas also badly needed the money Northerners were eager to invest in the new venture. Added to this was the demand for the beef which the Great White Father's social-security scheme needed to keep the Indians believing in barren idleness. This combination of factors set off a dissemina-tion of cattle unknown to any nation before or since.

North and west from Texas, the great herds fanned out like the writhing, sinewy tentacles of some gigantic beast bent on encompassing the world. Cattle by the thousands, by the millions, bound alike for markets and for new ranges wherever grass grew. Ten or fifteen miles a day, fording creeks, swimming rivers, crossing mountains, desert, and plain, and grazing their way to fatness while they moved.

This was the stage on which the cowboy inaugurated that great pageant of western romance which is with us to this day. Only his knowledge and skills could have shaped that fantastic panorama of wild-eyed longhorns and horses that obeyed no rules into a tightly knit production which embraced half a continent. From the Rio Grande to the Saskatchewan we see him, sitting his saddle day after day and month after month, heedless of rain, hail, snow, droughts, freezing northers, and searing winds off the Arkansas, Platte, and Yellowstone rivers. Fighting off hostile Indians and marauding white men, swimming the masses of stubborn, untamed brutes across rivers swollen by rain to twice their normal width, or riding down stampedes under storm clouds that turned the world into an inky void and sent lightning dancing crazily on the tips of tossing horns and horses' ears. On his horse from daylight to the guard change long after dark; using wit, ingenuity, and raw courage to handle situations that men of lesser mold would never have dared attempt. Campfire meals and a bed on the ground; perhaps a grave on stampede-churned ground or by the bank of some swirling lonely river. The stark, bold world of the cowboy, which only the cowboy could conquer or appreciate.

Colonel Charles Goodnight and Oliver Loving trailed a herd across the Staked Plains, over an unknown route, to Horsehead Crossing of the Pecos, then north to Fort Sumner, New Mexico, in 1866. Goodnight took another herd over the same route the following year, continuing on to Pueblo and Denver, Colorado. Some of these animals were driven on to John W. Illif's new ranch at Fremont Orchard, on the South Platte, that winter.

It was when Goodnight and Loving were outfitting for their 1866 drive that the former devised the original chuckwagon, with drop-board grub box on the rear end, which was to become so much a part of all range outfits in following years. Previous to the colonel's invention, the early cow outfits had used packhorses for this purpose.

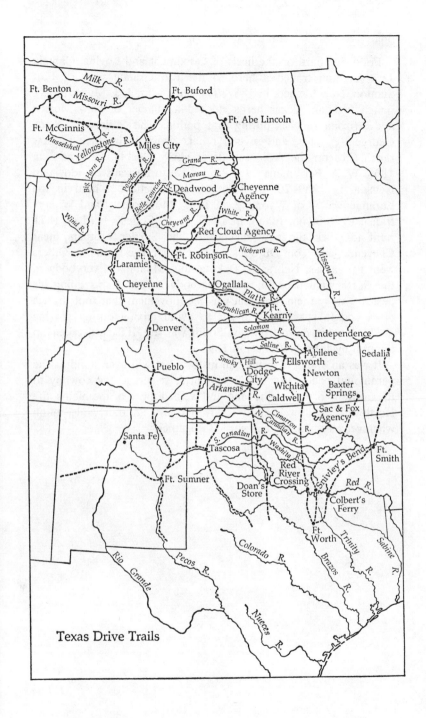

Texas Drive Trails

Following hard on the heels of Goodnight and Loving, Captain Jack Cureton trailed a herd to the Rio Grande west of Fort Stanton, New Mexico, in 1867. The same year, J. J. Myers took a bunch to Utah. Texas herds stocked a number of New Mexico and Arizona ranches during that period. The Pollard brothers, George Reynolds, and several others drove their stock to new ranch sites on the Arkansas River above Pueblo, Colorado, in 1868. W. A. Peril made a two-year drive to Lassen's Meadows, in Nevada, in 1869–70. Bullock and Mills settled a herd in the Laramie Valley of Wyoming, in 1868. Montgomery and Withers trailed to Branyon, Idaho, in 1870. C. F. Coffee's herd of 1871 went to stock the new ranches of the Snyder brothers, near Cheyenne, and Tom Durbin's Snake River range in Idaho. Others went to Kansas, Nebraska, Dakota, and Montana. Everybody in the North wanted cattle, and everybody in Texas was doing his best to supply them. So great was the movement that trail drivers often had to space their herds to avoid mixing during grazing

The last big drive from the South was an XIT herd taken up the trail by John McCanels in 1896.

It was an epoch in American history that will ever stand as the paramount pageant of the New World. It spread the cowboy to the farthest corners of the land and welded those of the plains, the Northwest, Southwest, and California into an indivisible union wherever men, horses, and cattle foregather.

*Chapter VII*

## UP THE TRAIL

Driving the great trail herds from five hundred to twenty-five hundred miles, often breaking new trails through a virgin wilderness that few white men had ever seen, was an art in itself. The cattle were almost as wild as their primitive ancestors. Anything might set them off in headlong stampedes. Beef-hungry Indians roamed everywhere, gaunt lobo wolves lurked in every covert, water and feed were uncertain, and flashing lightning and driving storms of rain or snow were ever-present threats to man and beast. There were rivers, turbulent from spring thaws, to be swum, and waterless deserts to cross with only hopes of unknown water-holes to look forward to. Mountain ranges offered precarious passage, and no guideposts marked the sucking quicksands and innocent-appearing bogs which lay in wait for the unwary.

Of course, after a couple of drives over any given route, the new trail could be more easily followed, in most cases. Information about the location of water, the best grazing, and worst danger spots would be passed down the line. Yet it was a wild, raw land. The men who conducted the big herds to distant markets or new ranges were strictly on their own. Success in delivering from one to three thousand head of the half-wild creatures to some spot two to six months' distant, with only the help of some ten or a dozen men, called for giants of nerve and self-sufficiency.

First, the herd had to be gathered and road branded in preparation for the drive. This was no little task in itself. All animals of the herd, often mixed stock belonging to several owners, must be marked with a single distinctive brand for identification while on the trail. As the drive usually started early in the spring, the branding crew more often than not found itself frequently plagued by cold spring rains as it plowed through the mud to rope, throw, and brand some three thousand full-grown steers, all violently opposed to the operation. There were seldom any corrals or branding chutes, as were known in later years. Such work had to be conducted in the open, with only ropes and horses to facilitate the task.

Then came another ten days or two weeks of almost continuous riding until the herd became trail broken. A green herd was always prone to scatter, break off in bunches, and create trouble in a score of ways. Stampedes were frequent, inveterate bunch-quitters had to be watched day and night, and even the more docile animals were likely to betray any misplaced trust until familiarized with the daily routine. During this initiative period, the men would ride all day, then half of them stand guard until midnight, when the other half took their places until daylight.

The guard duty would naturally be lightened after the herd became trail broken. Then, two men on duty during two-hour shifts were sufficient to handle the situation. These guards would ride in opposite directions around the bedded herd, meeting and passing each other at each circling of the resting animals. Much of the riding was done to the accompaniment of the low-toned range-songs, which commonly had a soothing effect on the beasts.

Dark, stormy nights, however, called out the whole crew to stand guard. When the herd was spooked up for an impending stampede, songs and soothing voices did little good. All anyone could do was hold them the best they could and pray for good luck.

Most stampedes took place under moonless skies, when the world was a black void. The savage fury of a sudden nighttime electrical storm created the most critical moments. Yet anything could start the wild flight. It might be a disturbed rattlesnake, the sudden flare of a match, the prodding of a restless steer, a bolt of lightning, or perhaps for no reason that could be determined. The first thing anyone would know, the entire herd would be on its feet and running with a thunder that shook the ground.

No man ever saw a herd of longhorns get to its feet in a stampede break. Unlike the measured lurching upright of ordinary cattle, longhorns made the transition in a single move. One instant they would be lying down; the next, the entire herd would be on its feet and running.

And how they could run! One herd stampeded near Dodge City in 1883. Fifteen hours later some of them were seen following the back trail across the Cimarron River, over 60 miles away. Another herd of five thousand steers stampeded north of the Platte River, in Nebraska, the following year. They quit their bedground at ten o'clock one Friday night. At 11 A.M. the following Sunday, the leaders made their appearance 120 miles to the south.

The only way a stampede could be handled successfully, if conditions permitted it to be done, was to force the runaway herd to run a circular course until the leaders caught up with the rearmost animals, then tighten the circle so that the animals were all milling around in a small space until fatigue quieted them.

And here was another peculiarity of the longhorns, absent in other cattle: When a stampede was turned into a mill, this breed always milled to the right. Old rangemen deny ever having seen a stampede mill to the left.

But however it was done and whatever the ultimate degree of success rewarded them, the cowboys stayed with the herd. If the critters could not be turned, it usually meant riding for unreckoned distances in the darkness of a stormy night, trusting fate and a pony's sense of footing to dodge badger and prairie-dog holes, water-gouged gullies, and sheer cut-banks. Morning might find any of these individuals miles away from the camp, with only a segment of the herd still with him. Or, as occasionally happened, some of his comrades might find him trampled into a bloody pulp in the mud. It was all part of the job. But no real cowboy ever quit trying until the cattle were stopped.

Should the herd be recaptured in a short while, by running them into a mill or otherwise, they were usually taken to a new bedground for the rest of the night. Here, they were less apt to break a second time than at the former place of disturbance. Placing them on a spot of ground higher than the surrounding territory was also an aid in this direction. But when a thoroughly spooked herd persisted in repeated stampedes, it was common practice to string them out and drive all night. Daylight would find them quieted down enough for the outfit to pull in for a much-needed rest without fear of further trouble.

One of the greatest stampedes on record took place in 1882, near the Red River Crossing at Doan's Store. Eleven herds, containing a total of thirty-thousand cattle, along with two thousand horses, were being held on the south side of the river, waiting for the high water to subside enough that they might cross. Then came a sudden terrific electrical storm. In the enveloping darkness, the already-restless cattle broke and ran. The horses also caught the spirit of the occasion. Daylight found all eleven herds and the two thousand horses scattered far and wide. And they were as thoroughly mixed as they were scattered. It took the 120 cowboys ten days to regather them and sort out all the respective herds.

In the ordinary routine of driving, the herd would be up and grazing by daylight. Following breakfast, they would be thrown onto the trail, the two point riders leading out on either side of the foremost cattle. It was their job to keep the herd pointed in the proper direction, a direction that was often determined by pointing the chuckwagon tongue at the North Star the night before. The various swing riders, half on each side of the herd, were staggered along its length to keep the animals in order. Should the critters start to bunch up or the line grow too thin, it was their responsibility to squeeze the line into a suitable width, or, if too much strung out, have the point men hold the leaders up until the desired width was restored.

These big herds would be in the neighborhood of half a mile in length. If allowed to travel in too great a width, they would move slower, and in hot weather the center animals often became overheated. A long, thin string would, conversely, move faster and usually handle more easily. But everything depended on the weather, the distance to next water, condition of grazing, Indian danger, and a multitude of other factors. A ten- to twenty-foot width for the whole herd was a fair average for ordinary driving conditions, although it might run up to fifty feet at times. It was the foreman's job to determine the best width for each day's drive and so order the crew. This width would be maintained until the next camp was reached, unless different orders were received.

The position of foreman required superior judgment and extensive knowledge of men, horses, and cattle, as well as nerve, daring, and a high degree of self-sufficiency. That many youths of eighteen to twenty years old served successfully as trail-herd foremen speaks volumes for the boys who grew up in the cowcountry.

The point riders were top-hands selected for their cow knowledge and skill. They retained their positions throughout the drive, save for changing sides each day because of the dust that always followed a moving herd. The swing men changed sides, as well as positions, each day. Thus, if there were four men on a side, the fourth, or last, one on the right side today would move up to number-three position on the left side tomorrow. When he had worked his way up to number-one position, he would drop back to the rear the following day and start all over again. This gave everyone an equal chance to get out of the dust every other day. It also allowed each to enjoy the lighter work common to the more advanced positions. The two or three drag, or rearmost, riders were usually older or steadier men who could be depended upon to keep the laggards in line and prevent any straggling.

It was the foreman who rode ahead each morning to locate the best water and grazing ground for the noon and night camps. The saddle-horse remuda and chuckwagon would follow him, so that meals and fresh horses would be ready when the herd reached the next stop.

Some uncharitable souls were fond of claiming that the boss liked to have the chuckwagon go on ahead so there would be less chance of the crew lagging along the way. Such opinions, however, are thought to border on heresy, as few real cowboys were ever known to shirk on a job once started.

Ten to fifteen miles was considered an average day's drive. In desert regions, however, it was not uncommon for the old longhorns to travel three or four days without water, graze, or much rest. The bulk of the driving would usually be done at night, in such cases. Stream crossings were preferably made before stopping for the night. The cattle were then more easily made to take the water. Too, one never knew when a flash flood from some higher region might make the stream impassable by the next morning, thus delaying the drive for an indefinite time.

Midday camp would be reached about eleven o'clock, when the herd would graze for an hour or two while everyone changed to fresh mounts and did justice to the cook's efforts. Then the drive would continue until an hour or so before sunset, when the herd would be again thrown off the trail to graze until bedding down at dark.

In throwing a herd off the trail, it was considered best to split the advancing column, turning one half each way from the trail as they came along. This made for speedier progress both when stopping for noon grazing and getting the animals back on the trail for resuming the march.

The nighthawk, or man who had charge of the horse herd at night, would take the remuda to a good grazing location, within reasonable distance from camp, as soon as the herd was bedded. It was his responsibility to see that none of the animals strayed away during the night. He caught up on his sleep between his jobs of rustling fuel for the cook's fire and driving the bed, or hoodlum, wagon between camps. This work was usually turned over to an apprentice cowboy making his first drive.

The daytime horse wrangler took charge of the remuda as soon as the nighthawk brought it in for mounting by the cowboys at daylight. During the day, he moved and grazed them to the next camp, herding them into the rope corral whenever a change of mounts was needed.

Altogether, the remuda would probably contain from sixty to one hundred or more horses for the wrangler to keep track of. Each cowboy would have from five to ten horses in his string. He usually needed three or four fresh mounts a day, besides a night horse for guard duty. In case of a stampede or other hard riding, he might use several mounts within the space of twenty-four hours. Then each man would probably have a favorite cutting horse and one especially adapted to roping. These were taken along for their special work, although seldom used for ordinary affairs.

All these special-purpose horses were necessary adjuncts to handling cattle. No successful cowman could do without such animals. The most skillful roper would be reduced to mediocrity without a knowledgeable horse under him. The best cowboy in ten counties might be made to look like an amateur if denied the use of a suitable cutting horse willing and able to outfox a cantankerous cow-brute. A gentle and dependable night horse was the best possible insurance against undue trouble with a bedded herd. Horses of these types were held apart for use in their particular fields and treated with marked respect. Ordinary riding was done mostly on the average run of common mounts.

Horses that have a natural bent for absorbing superior knowledge of a certain craft invariably enjoy their tasks. Some become so adept at their favorite work as to appear almost human in both thought and action. Among rodeo contestants, horses with outstanding ability in certain lines, especially roping and bulldogging, are valued at fabulous figures by their masters.

Such performances often bring to mind that old range classic about the two great cutting horses that met up in Montana.

It was along in the late '80s that one of the most famous cutting horses in Texas was taken north with a trail herd belonging to a certain outfit. Upon reaching the Montana ranch where the herd was to be delivered, the Texas boys soon found occasion to toss out some wide-range statements about their prize cutting horse. Unfortunately, they were met head on by the voice of Montana proclaiming that no horse ever lived who could outclass a well-known little brown gelding right there on the ranch. Neither outfit was given to bashfulness about its prize horse. It was but a matter of time until everybody's possessions were riding on the outcome of a contest set for the following Sunday.

Meanwhile, the two horses in question had been turned out on the range with the other extra saddle stock. It was arranged to bring them in to the ranch the day before the planned contest, so that there might be no hitch in proceeding.

Thinking it might be a neighborly gesture, a couple of the men, one from each outfit, decided on a trip to town the following day so that they might make a public announcement of the affair. Everybody in the country would appreciate having the chance to watch such a noteworthy match. Moreover, both Texas and Montana were eager for an audience to help applaud the superior performance of what each considered to be the better horse.

The two cowboys, still arguing amicably about the merits of

their respective animals, had only traveled a few miles in the direction of town when they heard a commotion going on behind a nearby uplift in the prairie. It sounded like somebody working cattle. With the thought of rustlers tickling their minds, the two left the trail to ride carefully up over the ridge.

What their eyes met from the summit set them both back in their saddles. There below them was a sizable herd of cattle which had apparently been rounded up by the two controversial horses themselves. And both of the animals were busily working the herd in a professional manner, cutting out the cows with calves from the mixed herd. The Texas horse was doing the cutting, while the Montana gelding held the cut off at a distance to one side. The cowboys watched spellbound as one cow after another was separated from the main bunch and shoved into the cut.

All was going smoothly until the Texan at last brought out a particularly salty old cow. He managed to get her safely to her destination; but the moment he turned away, she started trying to break back to the main herd. The Montana horse was forced to make several quick dashes to turn it back with the others. On its last attempt to have its own way, the Montana was led in a stern chase for several rods. Upon catching up with the critter, and now thoroughly exasperated, he clamped his jaws on its neck and bulldogged it to the ground. Then he sat down on its head until it decided to behave.

The properly humbled cow was later moving sedately back to her rightful place when the two cowboys backed their horses down off the ridge and returned to the ranch to tell their tale. Two such unbeatable champions, everyone agreed, surely rated equal honors without further demonstration, an opinion which still echoes whenever cowcamp sagas circulate.

Scarcely less bizarre are some of the factual accounts of longhorn wit and sagacity dealt with in another chapter. Many of these dot the annals of trail-driving days.

Most trail drivers used lead steers, which maintained their positions at the heads of herds throughout the long drives. Some of these might be called professionals, being retained for that purpose for many years. Many such animals became famous in cowcamp legends. Others might be particularly forceful and intelligent animals that simply worked themselves into the lead during a drive. But in any case, the lead steer invariably assumed and maintained his leadership in all the herd's movements for the duration of the drive. And woe be to any critter who tried to usurp his position. Good lead steers were of special value at stream crossings and in ticklish going, where the less-brainy animals, lacking such a leader, were prone to cause trouble.

Yet, despite the difficulties commonly encountered, these drives were not all on the seamy side. There was much fine weather, when all nature smiled and the unsullied green prairies rolled away to the farthest horizon in a vision of sheer beauty. Jokes and merriment took the edge off of many a trying moment; cowboys were ever a carefree lot. They habitually took their fun where they found it, burying all yesterdays under the promise of tomorrow. And for the owners, any fairly successful drive carried an enjoyable financial reward.

Ten-dollar Texas cattle ordinarily brought around thirty to thirty-five dollars per head at the railroad or on the northern ranges. Trail herds would average about three thousand head. Their delivery would call for ten or twelve cowboys, a foreman, wrangler, nighthawk, and cook. Grub for the outfit would run around a hundred dollars per month. With wages of a hundred dollars per month for the foreman and twenty-five to thirty-five dollars for the other men, the cost of the drive would average only about a dollar per mile for the entire trip. Barring a complete failure under exceptional circumstances, there was a rich harvest at the end of the trail for men of courage and spirit.

Such as they are the ones who are credited, by the best authorities, with taking between nine and ten million cattle and over a million horses up the trail during the 1865–95 period. Accompanying the herds were some thirty-five thousand men, thirty-five per cent of whom made repeated trips.

*Chapter VIII*

## MISSION CATTLE

In the Pacific Coast states, it was the missions which gave the first great boost to livestock raising. Following the early exploration of the West, all the missionary bodies were agog to sally forth and reap a harvest of souls in such a virgin territory. From all denominations they came, braving hardships and danger in their zeal to be first in any given region. Most of them were of the farmer-townsman class. All were convinced that the only way to salvation for all heathens was a thorough indoctrination in the beauties of hard work as applied to building fixed habitations and practicing agriculture. As one of the chief tenets of agriculture among a meat-eating people is the raising of livestock, the missionaries invariably included some cows as initial ingredients in the plan to keep their red converts from wandering away from home. The Indians, they reasoned, should be taught to raise their own beef, as well as the feed necessary for their welfare, and thus perhaps miss the benefits of higher civilization. In consequence, there were few of the mission establishments which lacked rapidly expanding herds by the middle 1800s.

California took the lead in thus sowing the seeds of cattledom along the coast. Thanks to the early efforts of Father Junípero Serra, the territory was overflowing with cattle before most of the others got started. From the few head the good padre brought north to stock his five original missions, in 1769–74, had risen a fabulous number of the animals. Mission San Gabriel alone had

30,000 head under its brand in 1826. A census of the collective mission herds of that state five years later totaled three hundred ninety-six thousand head. Besides that, they had supplied foundation stock for most of the new ranches which had been established between San Diego and San Francisco. And the cattle thus furnished for the latter owners had increased far in excess of those remaining at the missions. A single rancher, Diego de Ibarra, was to brand thirty-three thousand calves in 1856. Many other owners showed almost as impressive a figure during the 1830–50 period. California was selling fifty to eighty thousand dried cowhides annually to New England traders sailing around the Horn with trade goods.

Such hides were known to the trade as "California greenbacks." They brought the owners a dollar and a half to two dollars each on board the ships.

It was from these herds that the Pacific Northwest got its original start in cattle, as it likewise got its introduction to rangeland skills from the California vaquero.

Various writers of that period all refer to the cattle in the Columbia River territory as having come from Mexican and Californian stock. The first of these were four cows and two bulls brought to Nootka, on Vancouver Island, B.C., in 1790. Captain Vancouver mentioned seeing them there in 1792, as well as eight head across the strait at Neah Bay, Washington. It is a question if any of them survived after the Spaniards left. But whether they did or not, others were soon to follow.

Alexander Henry's journal for April 23, 1814, tells of two bulls and two heifers landed at Fort George (the former Fort Astor), at the mouth of the Columbia River, having been brought from San Francisco on the *Isaac Todd*. Peter Corney wrote that there were twelve head of cattle there in 1817. Figuring bred heifers to begin with and one hundred per cent calf crop, it would have been possible for this increase to have come from the original importation.

This appears to have been the stock which Dr. John McLaughlin acquired when he took charge of Fort Vancouver, at the present site of Vancouver, Washington, in 1825. Most of the other accouterments of Fort George were moved to Vancouver at that time. McLaughlin was interested in promoting cattle raising in his bailiwick, and he would have certainly grabbed up any foundation stock that was available. In a letter written by him in 1833, he stated that ". . . in 1824 we had only 17 cows besides what we supplied other places. Our stock of cattle is now between 400 and 450."

These had increased to a thousand head by 1837, according to William A. Slocum, who brought his ship up the Columbia that spring. Slocum also wrote that this stock came from the two cows and bull brought from California in 1814. The corresponding accounts by these most reliable reporters leave little doubts that the several references to Oregon's first cattle were all related to the same animals. And they present a definite picture of Spanish cattle being the first to populate the Northwest.

The remarkable advancement of McLaughlin's enterprise was due chiefly to his exemplary foresight and management. At the start, he decreed that none of the animals should be killed except one bull calf each year, for rennet to be used in cheese making. Later, he started the practice of lending cows to the various forts, missions, and the few settlers, mostly company employees who had retired to farms of their own. The borrowers received only the use of the cows for milk and work; the calves reverted to McLaughlin.

Under this arrangement, one or two cows were sent to Fort Okanogan and three to Fort Colville, on the upper Columbia, in 1826. Four went to Fort Langly, British Columbia, in 1832. Others evidently went to Fort Nisqually, on Puget Sound, and Forts Alexander and George, on the upper Fraser River. Lieutenant Johnson, who visited the latter places with the Wilkes Expedition of 1841, reported a seventy-cow dairy at Nisqually and small herds at the other forts. Colville, he said, had 196 head and Okanogan thirty-five. The few cows sent to Fort Nez Percé, at the mouth of the Walla Walla River, and Forts Boise and Hall, in Idaho, must have done equally well. At any rate, the missionaries Whitman and Spalding were able to trade five played-out cattle at Fort Boise for replacements at Fort Nez Percé in 1836. Eells and Walker did the same thing two years later, leaving fourteen head at Fort Hall in exchange for a like number to be obtained at Fort Colville.

It was not until 1836 that the first McLaughlin animal was killed for beef. Meanwhile, his plan had established cattle in the

Northwest as a going concern. At that time there were 1,000 head of live cattle and forty yoke of oxen at Fort Vancouver." This was exclusive of the rapidly expanding small herds at the various other forts. A McLaughlin letter of 1837 says they were able to kill forty head for beef that summer. Succeeding years saw greater returns from the seedstock allowed to mature.

Moreover, the healthy increase enabled Dr. McLaughlin to extend his lending of cows when the host of new missionaries and settlers began arriving in the Oregon country after 1836. The first of these, a bull and eight cows, went to the Reverend Jason Lee in 1835, as a keystone for his new mission at Salem, Oregon. Many later trailworn newcomers found the loan of a cow to be an invaluable asset in that first hard struggle for survival in a new land.

These animals were augmented in 1837 by six hundred thirty head of California cattle that the former mountain-man Ewing Young bought at San Jose and San Francisco missions and trailed north to the Willamette Valley. A further importation was made by Joseph Gale and Felix Hathaway in 1842, when they drove 1,250 head to the Willamette from San Francisco. Following years saw many more of the sturdy Spanish animals trailed north to the Oregon Territory.

This movement of California cattle into the Pacific Northwest was fairly contemporaneous with the seeds of progress being sown by the Texans east of the Rockies. The former has been somewhat lost sight of under the blaze of publicity given the larger Texas herds, which were so much more prominent in the view of advancing settlers and the literary East. Nevertheless, the cowmen of the West Coast were on the move for new grass and new markets with no less vigor than that of the Southerners.

We have seen how the efforts of Dr. McLaughlin and his mission friends gave the Northwest territories a widespread foundation stock of Spanish cattle from California. When the first American settlers arrived on the scene, it was these cattle which provided them with a nucleus for future herds and beef for the table.

Cattle have always stood in men's minds as nature's basic food staple. When later immigrants began to head for Oregon, they realized they were going into a virgin land, largely unpeopled and far removed from any source of purchasable commodities. In consequence, most of them took home-grown eastern animals with them, both as food insurance and the germ of future prosperity.

The first of these eastern importations to be of much consequence was the thirty-six head brought to the lower Columbia River region by the White-Hastings party of 1842. The Burnett-Nesmith-Applegate train of 1843 included ninety-four oxen and 8,000 head of loose cattle. Other outfits came equipped with proportionate numbers. Growing migration in the following years saw more and more herds trailed to the western valleys. The Oregon Territory census of 1850 gives a cattle population of 41,729. Ten years later, it had jumped to 182,382. These included several herds of top-quality shorthorns and similar heavy breeds. These larger and beefier eastern animals, mixed with the hardy, self-sufficient Spanish stock, produced a tough and sturdy breed of good size that made excellent range critters.

Settlement of the Northwest had, in the beginning, been in the warm valleys west of the Cascades. By the mid 1850s, rapidly growing herds were turning the eyes of cattle growers toward the grassy, high-plateau regions of eastern Oregon and Washington. This was a natural range country, big and open and without the heavy stands of timber found nearly everywhere on the west slope.

Ben Snipes laid the foundation of his great horse-and-cattle empire in the Yakima Valley of Washington during the spring of 1855. Mention is found of several Willamette Valley herds being moved into eastern Oregon in the late 1850s, but details are hazy. There is record of a rancher being already established in the Jordan Valley when he was killed and his stock run off by the Indians in 1863. That was the same year Doc Inskip's Ruby Ranch was founded in the same neighborhood. Others were on their trail. By 1865, new ranches were springing up all the way from the crest of the Cascades to Fort Hall, Idaho, and north to British Columbia.

It was from these newly established herds that beef was trailed north to the mining camps of the Caribou and Fraser River country of British Columbia, the Fort Colville region of Washington, and the gold fields of central Idaho during the 1858–67 period. Three hundred head of breeders from the Columbia went to the Flathead Indians of Montana in 1860. Many were driven to the gold camps around Virginia City, Montana, between 1860 and '70.

Then in the middle of the boom, the depression of the early 1870s fell on their heads. The mines started closing down everywhere. There were no markets in the West and no railroads to take the cattle East. Most of the cattlemen were already overstocked. The corresponding increase in the herds only made matters worse. It was much the same situation that had engulfed Texas a decade earlier. The economic toboggan was already nosing into the swift and deadly down-glide when the north-plains ranchers appeared over the horizon with money in their hands.

Several Montana cowmen had been given the opportunity to see the heavier, tick-free cattle of the West. These animals impressed them as superior to the rangy Texas longhorns for stocking the new ranges on the north plains. And they were cheaper. Word came back over the mountains that these better cattle, worth thirty-six dollars a head in Montana, could be bought for twelve to eighteen dollars in Oregon and Washington. Also, it was a much shorter drive than the long trail from Texas. The good news gained momentum. Before long, aspiring cowmen were packing their saddlebags with gold and heading for the Columbia, the Snake, and the Malheur.

General Wood wrote in 1875 that several Oregon herds had already reached Montana. Emsley Jackson helped with a herd that went to Cheyenne in 1876. The Frewen brothers stocked their Powder River ranch, in Wyoming, with Oregon cattle in 1878. Granville Stuart wrote that he brought one thousand head of Oregon stock to his Montana ranch in 1878. John Chapman trailed a herd to Pat O'Hara Creek, north of Cody, Wyoming, in 1879. A westbound emigrant of 1879 wrote of meeting three thousand Oregon cattle bound for the Yellowstone Valley.

By 1880, the movement was in full swing. All through these years, the western herds continued to multiply as the buckaroo trailed his surplus east to help repopulate the empty grasslands so recently denuded of the buffalo hordes. The Montana census of 1880 records the cattle brought into the state that year as 10,000 from Washington, 16,725 from Oregon, and 15,000 from Texas. Granville Stuart stated that 12,000 western animals were brought to his ranch alone between 1879 and 1883. One estimate, thought to be very conservative, numbered the Oregon-Washington cattle brought into Montana in 1885 at something over 40,000 head. Wyoming was not far behind. And many herds were trailed on through to the Dakotas during the same period.

Many of the characteristics which gave the West its great stature rode north from Texas on the backs of Spanish mustangs. A separate, but equally great, array of customs and traditions drifted up through the intermountain region from California. These two influences met and mingled on the plains and in the mountains of the North. Both were the product of big dreams, daring ventures, and great accomplishments. Most of the bold pageantry that was theirs found birth in the bawling trail herds that pounded out new paths across the western wilderness. Not a little arose from the exigencies of life in an untamed land met and conquered by sheer initiative and ingenuity. Together, they wrote a chapter of cowcountry history unique in itself.

It is the story of this assimilation of the two counterparts and the distinctive features which blended themselves into a single unit that has received all too little attention in popular western literature.

Omissions of this nature rose from purely natural causes. Without wishing to detract from the remarkable and far-reaching efforts contributed by the plainsmen during the early days, the fact remains that the northwestern buckaroos did fully as comparable a job in trailing untold thousands of Washington, Oregon, and Idaho cattle east to the north plains. The chief difference between the Texas trail driving and that from the Northwest was that the bulk of the northwestern driving came at a later date, mostly after 1880, and the buckaroo stirred up less commotion while doing it.

This last factor was due more to outside influence than to the men themselves. East or West, cowboys were very much the same —easygoing, hard-working, honest, and dependable, but possessing all the pride and temperament handed down by generations of nobility. Mutual respect allowed them to get along among themselves with a minimum of friction. It was when subjected to the machinations of alien minds born under the shadow of intolerance, greed, selfishness, and misunderstanding that they blazed forth in a wild and unpredictable manner.

The Oregon trail had little of this foreign provocation to contend with. Most of his routes led through unpeopled country, and there were no railroads to spill their riffraff in his path. In consequence, he went about his business in his typical orderly manner, meeting little that would dramatize him in the eyes of anyone looking for dead men scattered around in his wake like apples in the family orchard after a hard wind. This was in direct contrast to the parasitic growth which tended to force his plains cousin into the limelight at every railroad cowtown between Red River and Fort Benton. Moreover, the Westerner received little of the public acclaim that descended on the plains faction when eastern and foreign capitalists rushed forth to fatten on the rich harvests those early Texans had planted.

It was without fanfare or editorial headlines that knowledgeable cowman in the North turned toward the heavier and beefier northwestern cattle. They were cheaper, fattened quicker, and were free from the dreaded Texas fever tick. Also, settler expansion in Kansas and Nebraska was interfering with trail driving from the South. Many of the early trails were being cut off, while quarantine regulations were a problem in various sections. Though Texas herds were to come north for many years, their heyday was vanishing in the dust of their western rivals.

It was the bad winter of 1886–87 that started pulling down the curtains on this colorful era. Snow came early that fall. One storm followed another relentlessly. Frigid cold clamped down on the north plains, pinning an icy blanket over feeding grounds far and wide. Cattle died by the thousands from the Milk River to the Cimarron. A belated spring found many ranchers completely ruined. All of them were seriously crippled economically. Money was scarce and spirits were low. The big boom was over.

Then, on the heels of this catastrophe, the nester deluge began pouring its Niagara of sodbusters onto all the good grasslands from the Missouri to the Rockies. Equipped with sturdy rod breaking-plows and the new barbwire, first patented by J. F. Glidden, of De Kalb, Illinois, in 1874, they destroyed the open-range empire in less time than it took the hide hunters to butcher the buffalo.

There was virtually no trail driving from the West after 1890. Vanishing cattle buyers of the plains were replaced by the access to eastern markets provided by railroads advancing into the Northwest.

But it still graces the American scene as one of the most colorful dramas of the West. And it helped create an enduring industry which will ever portray itself on men's minds as that vast and enchanting land of wide horizons and great visions—the American cowcountry.

*Chapter IX*

## THE CHALLENGE OF CHANGE

During the great trail-driving days, both from Texas and the Northwest, there came into being assorted changes in riding equipment, clothing, and the like. Some of these improvements were developed by the cowboys themselves. Others were worked up by manufacturers and suppliers eager to capture the cowboy trade. Many of the new innovations withered on the vine under the cold eyes of independent men who accepted only what they found best suited to their needs. Old-time cowboys were never swayed by fashion's ballyhoo. On the other hand, no one was quicker to recognize and adopt a true betterment designed to their liking.

Along with this, when the southern cowboy met the northwestern buckaroo on the north plains, there inevitably occurred a great interchanging of ideas, customs, and practices between East and West. Though both were the same breed of men, following the same line of work in a similar fashion, each had his own peculiarities unique to the region in which he had been trained. Their assimilation and reciprocal adaptation of each other's methods worked to the advantage of both.

The western buckaroo was a dally-man, the same as the California vaquero. His Yankee-born love of invention, combined with the Spanish desire for finer things, had, however, led him to develop the high-forked saddle with tall, slender horn as best suited for the practice of taking quick turns of the rope around the horn. At the same time, he rigged it with a single centerfire cinch that he found adequate and more convenient for the type of work prevailing on the western ranges. Then he worked a further improvement by attaching the rigging straps to the tree underneath the skirts. This gave a much neater appearance than the old Mexican style of exposed rigging.

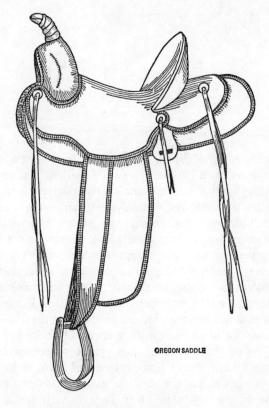

OREGON SADDLE

By the time he reached the Oregon country he had pretty well discarded the vaquero's braided rawhide rope. The increase of sailing ships and overland transportation to the Pacific Coast, after 1850, brought a growing supply of fiber rope, made at Plymouth, Massachusetts, for the maritime trade. First introduced by visiting seamen, it won a great and lasting preference over the native reatas by most Americans.

Much of this was due to the fact that not everyone could make first-class rawhide ropes. It was an exacting craft. Few Americans cared to devote the time necessary for such a painstaking job. Furthermore, the braided rawhide was more subject to damage from dampness, unyielding jerks, rock cuts, and other causes than was the hemp variety. American leadership during ensuing years led to an almost total change in the roper's chief tool.

On the other hand, long familiarity had created in the buckaroo a strong liking for the short, square or rounded saddle skirts used by the Californios. He switched to the American bent-wood stirrups at an early date, but, to a large extent continued covering them with the long Mexican tapaderos. He also favored the lightweight California bridles, big Spanish bits with spade or ring mouth-pieces, and the musical tinkling of jingling bit chains.

Too, he clung to the big and elaborately decorated Spanish spurs, which, unlike the plainsman, he commonly removed when dismounted. This practice was a hangover from the early California days, when the vaquero's footwear consisted of moccasins or poorly made shoes. Without either high boot heels or stiff counters to hold the long-shanked, big-roweled conquistador spurs high on the heel, their ground-dragging propensities made them rather awkward accouterments when afoot. The Californio solved the problem by simply taking them off whenever he dismounted. Later generations merely perpetuated the habit as a fixed custom of the country.

Even today, over two centuries after the vaquero first preempted the California valleys, his heavy and ornately decorated spurs still to a large extent identify the western rider. Shanks remained fairly long, usually formed with graceful curves and modified rowels up to two and a half inches in diameter.

The turned-up heel bands and swinging buttons were innovations adopted from east of the Rockies around the turn of the century; such designs never appeared among the original Californios. While later years have seen a still-greater intermingling of regional peculiarities, the old basic differences in this badge of the horseman remain to mark the home range of most cowboys.

Similar sectional needs and traditional customs provided the evolutionary stimulus for many other practices which set the western buckaroo apart from his blood cousin across the mountains.

The former seldom used quirts, a plains item inherited from the Indians. Buckaroos preferred their romal-type reins, which served much the same purpose. They also liked the big saddlebags, which often were covered with angora goat skins to match their chaps. The closed-leg angora chaps were very popular throughout the Northwest, especially for winter wear.

Hackamores, seldom seen elsewhere in the early days, were very prevalent on the Pacific slope. The western vaquero and his American successor always had a penchant for soft-mouthed horses. Hackamores were commonly employed for breaking the young animals, bits being used after they became bridle-wise. This was in direct contrast to the plains custom of doing the breaking with bits and reserving the hackamores, when they were used at all, for bridle-trained horses. With their hackamores, the buckaroos customarily used a ten- or twelve-foot rope, often of twisted hair, tied to the back end of the bosal, or noseband. The knot used in tying could be made to exert pressure under the animal's jaw, thus serving as an excellent control measure. Doubled back on itself, it might be used as a pair of reins. It was also suitable for holding or tying the horse when dismounted.

These western riders seldom practiced ground tying their horses, as did the plainsmen. When hackamore ropes were not present, they would tie with the reins. This seems to have been due mainly to the long-established California custom of using rather short, closed reins. These were not very suitable for being allowed to drag under a horse's feet.

The plainsman's long, open reins would not become seriously entangled under shifting hoofs. The sharp jerk usually resulting from an animal stepping on one of these dragging members more often served as a gentle reminder to stand tied. The average plains horse was well trained in this practice. It commonly held its position as though tied solidly to a post, so long as the reins were on the ground. Such a method had considerable virtue in prairie country, where anything larger than a sunflower stalk might not show itself within fifty miles. It also saved many a long walk when riders were inadvertently thrown or set afoot far from camp.

Neck reining, on the other hand, was invariably practiced by all cowboys, East or West. An inheritance from old Spain, it offered the best and most satisfactory method in existence for guiding cowhorses. A mere touch of the rein drawn across a mount's neck would serve to turn the animal instantly, while at the same time exerting no hard pressure on the customary severe bit. This method also permitted use of the big, half-breed, spade and ring bits, so often useful in controlling the wild and unpredictable mustangs, without working any damage on the beast's mouth unless necessity demanded such action. Thus, most cowhorses quickly learned the threatened, but seldom used, punishment of harsh bits, and answered immediately to any slight movement of the reins against its neck.

No less peculiar to the buckaroo was his custom of folding the saddle blanket small enough that only a scant edge showed below the saddle skirts. His counterpart east of the Rockies took the opposite view, by folding his blanket so that a generous, and usually colorful, edge was left exposed.

It was also the Westerner who first popularized the close-fitting, blue-denim Levi's, which young Levi Strauss had devised for the miners at Sacramento. These trousers were in the nature of a rebirth of the tight undergarments once worn by armor-clad knights. When the knights shed their armor, they, like all succeeding horsemen, continued to favor smooth, tight-fitting garments that would not bunch or wrinkle under the seat or legs. As few manufacturers at that time were interested in cowboy clothing, the Californio was about the only one who had pants suitable to his calling. The American vaquero had a natural aversion to rigging himself up in Mexican costume, so he was forced to make out with whatever he could get. He often didn't get much. At the best, it was usually of an unsatisfactory nature. It remained for the arrival of the twenty-year-old Strauss in California, with a supply of unsalable canvas, to provide the full answer.

It was in 1850 that this newcomer showed up in Sacramento. Nobody was about to go home at that stage of the game, so the canvas Strauss had hoped to sell for wagon covers found no buyers. He was almost reduced to digging gold or going hungry when he chanced to meet a miner decrying the impossibility of finding a serviceable pair of pants in the new settlement.

The encounter exploded a sudden blinding light before Strauss's eyes. He immediately set about turning some of his unwanted canvas into a pair of pants sewed up with harness thread. The creation proved to be just what the miner had in mind. In a matter of hours, the man's voice was heard all over camp, proclaiming the superlative quality of those wonderful pants of Levi's.

From there on, it was all downhill for the pantsmaker. When his canvas ran out, he switched to a heavy blue denim and located a distinctive orange thread with which to do his sewing. This, by the way, was the only change ever made in the original design, with the exception of the copper-riveted pocket corners. The latter innovation arose from the troubles of another miner, by the name of Alkali Ike.

Strauss's booming business had given birth to a factory in San Francisco and several retail stores throughout the mining country. One of the stores, under the management of Jacob W. Davis, was located in Alkali Ike's home town of Virginia City, Nevada. Ike was much addicted to always having his pockets stuffed with ore samples. Such burdens were uncommonly hard on pockets. Every time Ike came to town, it was with uncharitable remarks about pantsmakers and a demand to have his flapping pockets resewed.

Good businessman that he was, Davis always obliged by rectifying this apparent weakness in his product. But just as repeatedly, Ike would show up with the same complaints. Davis's patience finally wore thin and, partly in exasperation and partly as a joke, he took Ike's pants over to the harness shop and had the harnessmaker rivet the corners of the pockets with square-cut nails.

It was a joke the whole town enjoyed while Ike made his way homeward, too drunk to evaluate the nature of his new repairs. The joke backfired, however, a few days later. Davis woke up to find himself besieged by a humble and serious demand from all the miners that they should be equipped with similar riveted pockets. A hasty consultation with Strauss found the latter again quick to see the handwriting on the wall. He helped Davis acquire a patent on the idea soon afterward. Together, in the late 1860s, they made the riveted pockets a standard feature of the popular Levi's, the copper type being chosen to avoid rust stains.

The cowboy, who had long been wanting comfortable and durable clothing suitable to his needs, soon saw what the miner had discovered and promptly took it for his own. As he moved northward into the Columbia River basin, and later across the continental divide, we find him clothed in those copper-riveted pants of Levi's. He had also discarded the Mexican-type jacket for one of the same blue denim, short and snug-fitting, bearing the same copper-riveted pockets.

This notable contribution to the culture of the West had come of age. Outdoor workmen the world around found it to be the paramount answer to their everyday needs. As the cowboy settled himself in every part of the awakening West, he promptly adopted Levi's as the standard wear for the ultimate in saddle comfort, durability, strength, looks, and protection. He also used them to stuff cracks in bunkhouse walls, tie up calves, mop floors, blindfold horses, tow stranded vehicles, or any of the hundred and one other things that called for a soft, strong, and pliable material.

Charles C. Ashurst of Los Angeles even tells of how, when firing a locomotive in Arizona in 1899, he and the engineer soused the latter's Levi's in the water tank and then twisted them into a rope to replace a broken coupling link between the tender and the first car. He said the pants held during the remaining ten miles to Flagstaff, despite several stiff grades. The improvised Levi's coupling brought the seven loaded cars into town behind the old wood-burner without any further trouble.

One old cowboy wrote a letter to the company, complaining about the poorer material they were putting into their Levi's in later years. He said his last pair had come through in first-class shape for fifteen years; but the new ones, which he had worn only ten years, were already beginning to go.

As with Colt's revolvers and Stetson's hats, users the country over have made the name of Strauss's Levi's synonymous with cowboy pants. In a like manner have western writers and illustrators clothed their characters in Levi's for the best part of a century.

Incidentally, with the fashion world's post-World War II trend toward western fashions, Levi's have become the standard outdoor wear for both men and women throughout the country. And, as the rest of the world has come to view the cowboy as the exemplification of America, some sixty-five foreign countries now provide Levi's sales outlets so that their peoples may feel a touch of kinship with our storied West. A mural of this "Legend of the Old West" is now on display at the Dulles International Airport, Washington D.C., having been voted one of the sixteen American products of greatest interest to foreign visitors. Who is to say that this is not an equally glowing tribute to the men who were ever prone to map their own trails in both thought and action—the American cowboys.

It is the Northwest's buckaroo whom we must credit with bringing this new garment north from California, introducing it into the north-plains country as he followed the big herds east to Montana, Wyoming, and the Dakotas. Further influence of the Californio is still present in the small square or rounded saddle skirts, the tall, slender horn, and the centerfire rigging. Bits and spurs reflect the heritage of old Spain in their elaborate design, fancy carving, and silver inlays. Under his soft wool hat is the knowledge handed down by half a hundred centuries of westward-bound stockmen.

East of the Rockies, the same sort of progress was in motion. The Texan was pushing steadily northward to distribute his multiplying herds and establish new ranches. As he advanced toward the north plains, an ever stronger American influence entered into his outfit and customs. The old rawhide reatas had also given way almost entirely to the good, hard-twist fiber ropes from the East, as had happened on the west slope. He had modified the big Spanish spurs to a size more agreeable to his taste, although he retained most of their embellishments and pleasing designs. The big spade and ring bits had largely vanished in favor of the less severe half-breeds and roller-port Shoemaker types. Even his clothing was patterned mostly on American designs.

Along in the late 1860s, he took the old mochila-tree covering and made it into an integral part of the saddle. This became known as the Mother Hubbard saddle, which was to retain its popularity until late in the century. Then his Yankee inventiveness turned to strengthening the forks of his saddles. His own designs, which evolved from the old vaquero rigs, were often homemade of natural tree forks and rawhide. Unfortunately, heavy roping had a way of stretching them out of shape or pulling them apart. He finally counteracted most of this trouble by extending the front rigging up over the fork and taking a turn around the horn. With the new double rigging he had devised, this additional feature tied everything down in a secure unit that centered all the pull on the cinches. Whether on the end of a rope or screwed onto the back of an outlaw mustang, this saddle was hard to dismember or dislodge so long as the rigging held together.

Such saddles, however, lacked considerably in comfort and quality. A. C. (Teddy Blue) Abbott wrote that most of them in use during the 1860–70 period were sadly addicted to chewing up horses' backs and men's pistol pockets. Trees often split or warped; some caused kidney sores because of being overlong. Rawhide was prone to stretch and curl when alternating between dampness and hot suns. Cantles were frequently ill-shaped, skimpy fenders chafed the legs, and narrow, slick forks were lacking in comfort and security. It was not until 1882 that plains-country saddles developed into that splendid creation familiar to later cowboys.

To give this saddle its proper persective, we must turn back to before the Civil War. It might be considered a shining example of the gods grinding slowly but exceedingly fine. General Ulysses S. Grant had a hand in it, as did a pioneer Illinois saddlemaker, a U.S. senator, several high-ranking politicians, the U. S. Indian Bureau, and the American electorate of 1868.

A man by the name of Eli Collins was the first link. The father of two sons, John S. and Gilbert M., he was operating a saddle-making shop at Galena, Illinois, in the early 1800s. Some years prior to the outbreak of the Civil War, he had formed a partnership with a friend by the name of Jesse R. Grant, who had been operating a tannery at Georgetown, Ohio. The Collins boys were then working in the family shop, learning the saddlemaking trade from their father.

Grant's son, Ulysses, had meanwhile forsaken the pungent odors of tannery vats for an appointment to West Point and entry into the army. After winning some renown in the Mexican War and serving a few years on the western frontier, he resigned from the army in 1854. After starving out on a Missouri farm, he moved back to Galena and went to work in the Collins shop. It was there that the outbreak of war found him anxious to rejoin the cavalry.

But Grant was an independent, headstrong sort of individualist. He refused to sign up unless given a command. He figured that his previous service entitled him to a command post, and he probably harbored a few ideas about the coming conflict which only a ranking position could prevent from being buried. At any rate, he took his stand. And the army's attitude toward independent thinking being what it generally is, they took his application and filed it away in a dark corner.

Things rocked along until June without his being able to get any satisfaction in the matter. Grant was still chewing away on his fingernails when Eli Collins decided to deal himself in on the affair.

Collins had taken quite a liking to his partner's son, seeing in his hard-headed stubbornness a number of desirable qualities. Tired of the army's stalling tactics, he took up the matter with some of his upper-bracket political friends—Collins was something of a political figure himself. In the end, he went over to Springfield and put the case up to Senator Washburn. He evidently made his point. Shortly afterward, Grant was offered command of a hardcase Illinois regiment that no one else cared to tackle. That suited Grant just fine. So he went ahead and won the war.

Grant never forgot how his old friend Collins had helped him gain his objective in the army. It was this gratitude which prompted him to call in young John Collins, soon after he was elected to the Presidency, and offer him an ambassadorship in Europe. John, however, had no desire for striped pants and a clawhammer coat. He wanted to go out West, where he was associated with his brother, Gilbert, in a saddlemaking shop at Omaha, Nebraska. The upshot of the conference was that they settled on John taking the concession of post trader at Fort Laramie, Wyoming, instead of the higher position.

Collins assumed charge of his new duties in December 1872. Three years later, he found himself also appointed secretary of the Sioux Indian Commission.

Meanwhile, the Collins brothers had been busy with the saddle-making business they had established in 1864. Their ambition was to make not only the best saddles on the market, but the best saddles anyone could want.

At this time, people were becoming aware of the great year-round range possibilities in the North. Had not Seth Ward's oxen made it through in first-class shape after being turned out in the Laramie Valley during the winter of '52? Alexander Majors, the great freighting tycoon, had enjoyed the same experience with three hundred head of oxen in the same region two years later. Captain W. F. Raynolds wintered seventy army horses and mules over on Deer Creek in 1859. In the late 1850s, Uncle Jack Robertson, out in the Fort Bridger country, had been making a business of buying worn-out cattle from Oregon Trail emigrants and selling them at a huge profit to needy travelers the following year, after having fattened them up on the sun-cured grass along Black's Fork of Green River. Other individuals in western Nebraska and the Dakotas had found similar success in range feeding.

The Collins boys took a long look at the speculative cattle empire which men of the North were beginning to vision. What they saw there convinced them that one of the greatest needs in opening this new wilderness would be saddles suitable to hard-riding cowmen.

The Texan had not yet come north with his big trail herds and new saddle developments. There were a few of the old Spanish rigs from Santa Fe scattered around, but most riders had to depend on the hornless, flat-seated army and eastern-type saddles. These were practically worthless for roping and general range work. The Collins brothers carefully assessed the coming needs and prepared to meet the issue in a manner satisfactory to all.

Fortunately, John's appointment to the Fort Laramie post at such an opportune time placed them in a position to accomplish their main ambition.

The office of post trader at this particular fort was a very lucrative position. Whether or not it offered a chance for undue profits is no special concern of ours. All we know is that John accumulated a considerable fortune before resigning the job in 1877. And it was this money which made possible the early creation of that long-sought combination of adaptability to any range task and comfort for horse and rider—the cowboy's stock-saddle.

But even with the aid of luck's round-about financing, it was a long and difficult task. A whole new concept of tree designing had to be brought into play; new construction ideas were tried and discarded; newer and better materials were found. Only imagination and experimentation could find the answers. Only trial and error could determine the best shape for cantles, the best method of fastening horns to forks, the best style of rigging to insure security on the end of a rope or the back of a fighting mustang.

Many sample saddles were donated to rangemen in exchange for their reports on any shortcomings or suggestions for improvements they found in actual experience through the roughest of range work. This led to much altering, tearing down, and often starting all over on a new concept so that the necessary corrections might be made in future productions. Many of the early designs went into the junk pile.

It was a costly process, both in time and money. Between the cowboys' exacting demands and their own desire to satisfy the most discriminating taste, they fought a hard battle. It was not until 1882 that they succeeded in turning out the finest saddles anyone could want for any purpose.

All this is not to imply that the Collins brothers were alone in building fine saddles. The West was full of excellent saddlemakers, many of whom developed improvements that made the western saddle what it is today. Yet it was the original Collins creation which first launched the cowboy into a new era of comfort and security.

But to get back to the cowboy himself: He rode through this period, slowly creating and developing his various needs as he went along. Although a first-class saddle was his chief requirement, secondary equipment was equally essential.

Saddles could not give their best service without suitable cinches, so he worked his way up through rawhide straps, tanned leather bands, woven or twisted hair, and fabricated webbing until he found the soft cotton cords that offered the most security without chafing or galling a horse.

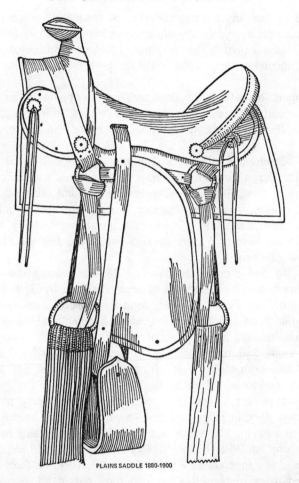

PLAINS SADDLE 1880-1900

He did the same with his stirrups, gradually moving on from the old Mexican wood-block type to the big and bunglesome box-car style, then to the neater oxbows. Iron models were used to some extent, but most cowboys cared little for them.

The Texan liked to cover his stirrups with tapaderos, graduating from the old Mexican box-nose type to the plain leather style, with dropping tips, around 1865. These were the favorite model all through the Southwest and up into the central plains.

In the North, the absence of thorn brush and heavy cactus

worked against any general adoption of tapaderos. Some riders liked them for everyday use, while others kept them only for bad-weather supplements. The majority, however, considered them useless encumbrances suitable only for parades and display out-fits.

Cruppers followed the Mexican saddles into oblivion at an early date, appearing thereafter only on packsaddles. Martingales and breast collars disappeared almost as completely in the cowboy world.

Thus, developing, altering, and improving his outfit as he went along, the Texan spread his folkways to the farthest reaches of the north plains. And although his forces were augmented by countless kindred spirits from other regions during later years, all as-similated themselves into that basically unchangeable body which came up the long trail from Mexico before the Pilgrim Fathers ever saw America.

Here we find him in the dawning 1880s, wearing the neat-fitting boots with high, underslung heels, designed by H. J. Justin at Spanish Fort, Texas, in 1878; John B. Stetson's new-style hat with curled brim and high crown, which had replaced the earlier plainsman model; heavy gauntlet gloves, their cuffs decorated with a Lone Star or a sunflower blossom and carrying leather fringes the length of the seams; fringed shotgun chaps, and a red bandanna tied loosely about his neck.

His well-perfected, double-rigged plains saddle—forty pounds for forty dollars, in range parlance—assures him that he can stay on top of anything that wears hair or hold on to anything he can dab his loop on. With the inevitable yellow slicker tied behind the cantle and his rope coiled against the saddle fork, he feels fully equipped to carve himself a cattle barony out of an untouched wilderness, in defiance of all opposition of man, beast, weather, or the contrarities of nature.

*Chapter X*

## THE ALL-AMERICAN COWBOY

It was in the beginning of the 1880s that the southwestern plains-man joined hands with the northwestern buckaroo to form that indivisible figure who stands before the world as the all-American cowboy. The characteristics which set this individual apart from his predecessors arose from a neat blending of East and West into a superstructure of his own devising. And it was his innovations in cowboy life and equipment that later flowed south to form a solid pattern throughout the West.

The first, and perhaps the most important, development to stem from this union was the Montana three-quarter saddle. The Texan had brought his double-rigged plains saddle with him when he came north. With it, he had set a pattern throughout the north plains while establishing his new ranges. But he had scarcely more than gotten himself comfortably settled before Oregon started trailing its herds east to the same territory. The latter was aboard his smaller-skirted, single-rigged centerfire saddle. The two met head on in Wyoming and Montana, about 1880. Their separate ideas on proper saddles were somewhat leavened by a generous assortment of individuals recently turned to cow work from the old days of hide hunting, beaver trapping, and association with the Indians.

These men, along with a scattering of ex-cavalrymen, had a strong dislike for the double-rigged outfits. Neither were they overly enthusiastic about centerfire rigs. Their views ran toward a modified design employing the single-cinch principle, similar to the way they had reworked the rigging on old Santa Fe and Indian saddles. At the same time, the Oregonian allowed that the heavy plains model would be a right good rig if they'd throw away that extra cinch. The Texan, in turn, recognized the good

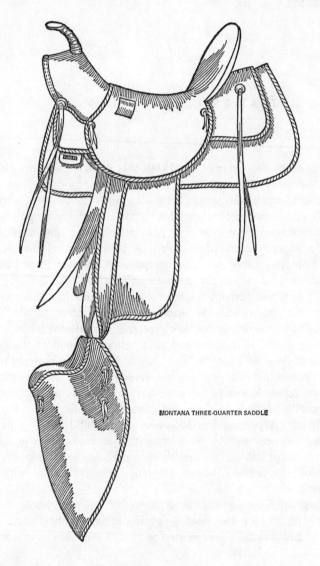

MONTANA THREE-QUARTER SADDLE

qualities of the western saddle in a country where excessive roping was seldom demanded; but he didn't like the latter's tendency
to crawl forward on low-withered horses or the more frequent
incidents of ring sores. In the end, these two absolved their differences on the common meeting ground of the mountain-men to
give birth to the distinctive Montana three-quarter rig.

This new saddle, which appeared in the Miles City area of Montana during the 1890–91 period, was of mixed design, built with a
single cinch set three quarters of the way forward. It carried the
high fork and straight, bound cantle of the Oregon saddle and the
square skirts of the plains model. The buckaroo frowned on the
plainsman's Cheyenne roll cantle, while the plainsman held a poor
opinion of the buckaroo's abbreviated skirts. The compromise
commonly exhibited the plainsman's lack of excessive carving
and ornamentation, while copying the Oregonian's covered rigging
and trimness of design. Narrow oxbow stirrups with leather
treads predominated. The brass-bound Visalia stirrups appeared
quite frequently, along with a scattering of the leather-covered
iron types. Iron stirrups, however, never won much favor in cold
regions of the North.

The north-plainsmen, in general, found great satisfaction in this
new saddle they had created. It not only became very popular
throughout that territory, but within a short time spread progres-
sively from the Missouri River to the Cascade Mountains and
south to Oklahoma and southern Colorado. The Southwest alone
clung to the old double-rigged outfit. The Montana three-quarter
did not show up among the southern cowboys until after 1910.

Meanwhile, the Miles City region had developed the five-eighths
rigging around 1900. This had the cinch set midway between the
centerfire and three-quarter positions. Possessing certain advantages and disadvantages, according to whose opinion you listened
to, it won a good measure of popularity. Although it has stood the
test of time, it has never attained the general favor of the three-
quarter.

Closely following these innovations, the newly blended cowboy began giving more consideration to the short, round, Cali-
fornia-style skirts. They were lighter in weight and more convenient to handle, and were less subject to warping and curling
at the corners. Shortly after the turn of the century, he began

incorporating this feature into his Montana-type saddles. The new adaptation soon won wide acceptance on the north plains. Oregon's nickel horn was also received with considerable favor east of the mountains.

The Northwest met the Montana develoments with reciprocal acclaim. From there, the new design worked its way south to merge with the original California round-skirted, centerfire rig, now embellished with a new steel fork developed at Sacramento in 1883.

It was this new saddle which moved east from California, as it had south across the plains. Around 1920, the two jaws of the pinchers closed on Texas. With various modifications and occasional reversals to the old sectional styles in certain regions, the hybrid creation of East and West, like the mixture of East and West cowboy himself, took its place throughout the rangelands as the typical Western stocksaddle.

And although the next great improvement in saddles saw life in Oregon, its original conception took place among the plains cowboys. This was the invention of the swell fork. Victor Marden of The Dalles, Oregon, was the first to bring out a saddle with built-in side bulges on the fork. His creation, developed in 1904, was designed as an improvement on the detachable bucking rolls patented by John Clark of Portland, Oregon, in 1900.

Clark's idea, however, as well as Marden's later development, was based on the old plainsman's habit of tying a coat or blanket roll across the pommel of his narrow, slick-fork saddle as anchorage for his knees and protection of vital anatomy from unyielding saddle horns when riding explosive mustangs. Thus the early makeshift adaptation of the south-plains saddle joined with the Montana saddle to reach its full stature at the hands of an Oregon craftsman. California soon added its distinctive touches, after which it traveled both east and south to its place of beginning on the southern plains.

Within little over one decade, the southwestern vaquero, northern puncher, plains cowboy, and Oregon buckaroo rode across the face of the West in the form of a single individual—the worldrenowned all-American cowboy.

Incidentally, while we are on the subject of fine saddles and American craftsmen, we cannot overlook the elaborately decorated specimens that have flashed across the western firmament from time to time. Of course, the world's upper-class horsemen have always gone to great lengths in acquiring ornate gear of the most costly nature ever since saddles were first invented. In early America, the old Spanish dons lavished extravagant care in choosing the finest leather carving and silverwork for their saddles. Many cowboys and vaqueros likewise invested most of their negotiable wealth in showy outfits. While much of this elaborateness declined considerably during the pioneer era of little money and few manufactured goods, the later economic development, higher wages and rise of western ranching, revived it in all its old-time glory.

The cowboy's innate pride and love of colorful accouterments, combined with regional celebrations, parades, and rodeos, has always called out his best efforts at making a striking and pleasing appearance. Early rodeos catered to this desire by offering highly decorated saddles, spurs, bits, and the like as prizes. Many of these prize saddles were masterpieces of the leather carver's and silversmith's art, running into hundreds of dollars. Objects of envy indeed were the men and women whose skill and daring won them possession of such creations.

Along with these were various affluent individuals who, with an eye to imposing appearances, outfitted themselves with highly embellished rigs of a similar nature. Important positions, desire for personal recognition, or the old human urge to be the brightest flower in the field led assorted horsemen to great heights of extravagance in obtaining the finest-designed outfits to be had.

Among the many such superior examples to claim public attention was the ten-thousand-dollar saddle made for Joe C. Miller of the famous 101 Ranch in Oklahoma. Designed and manufactured by that premier saddlemaker Sam D. Myers of El Paso, Texas, in 1914, its cost would equal a figure many times that size today. Mr. Miller had, at that time, made a very exhaustive study of saddle history, with the object of having a rig built that would surpass anything ever seen in that line. The resultant achievement is still considered by many to be the finest saddle ever produced.

It was made of the finest-quality leather throughout, built on a specially constructed tree. Its decorations consisted of 166 diamonds, 120 sapphires, 17 rubies, 4 garnets, and 15 pounds of sterling silver and gold. All the leather was hand-carved in exceptionally fine scroll effects. The fenders were finished with carved longhorn steer heads surrounded by butterflies. The initials J.C.M. were stamped on the front of the cantle, while the back was covered with a solid shield of silver, in the center of which was the 101 brand inlaid in gold. The 0 of the brand contained a solid gold star highlighted by a ruby in its center and fifteen diamonds outlining its five points. The horn was of chased gunmetal decorated with silver inlays in colors. It was crowned with a diamond brooch in horsehead effect set with seventy stones. Corners of the jockeys and housings displayed silver wreaths surrounding five-pointed stars, the wreaths being embedded with sapphires, while garnets formed the star centers and diamonds their points. Skirt corners carried similar wreaths of silver, each surrounding a solid gold steer head with diamond eyes and ruby nostrils. Five gold stars set with rubies and diamonds encircled each steer head. The fork and cantle bindings were of silver engraved in wreath designs. Silver plates with the 101 brand inlaid in gold covered the fork swells. The stirrups were covered with silver shields, each having a large rosette in its top center, where the gold 101 again appeared. It was, and is, a truly magnificent work of art, a worthy tribute to the romantic glamour that always rode with the pioneer plains cowmen.

There have been many saddles of this type made for outstanding individuals. Most were less elaborate, but still remarkable for their beauty and cost. The only logical reason for us not seeing more of them is the habitual lean condition of most cowboys' purses.

Fancy saddles of this type, however, have always been rather like the frosting on the cake: they added little nourishment to the main ingredients. To the working cowboy, a good serviceable saddle was the main requirement. Equipped with his new swell-fork rig, the average rangeman figured the gods had dealt him a flush hand. It remained for the saddlemakers to show him there were other cards in the deck.

Some of the boys tried to take matters into their own hands by having their saddles made with bigger and wider swells. Some of these ran up to twenty-two inches in width. The majority, however, stuck within the fourteen- to seventeen-inch range, which was found by experienced hands to be the most practical size for general-purpose work.

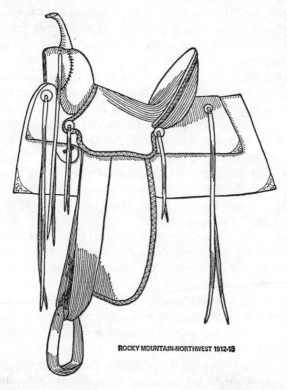

ROCKY MOUNTAIN-NORTHWEST 1912-13

A widespread favorite came out of the Northwest in the 1913–14 period. It had a rather low fork with a fourteen- to sixteen-inch swell and a leather-wrapped horn slanted slightly forward. Skirts were short and round, and it carried either of the three types of single rigging. It ran a close popularity race, in the northern Rockies and north plains, with the square- or round-cornered model favored by many riders during that period. Both are still well liked by working cowboys, the round skirts predominating on the west slope and the square ones across the mountains.

Another great favorite is the Form Fitter type, first designed by the Hamley Company of Pendleton, Oregon, in 1914. Many cowboys consider this the greatest development since the swell fork first came in.

Although the Association saddle, designed by L. H. Hamley and officers of the Rodeo Association in 1919, for bronc-riding contestants, and the low roper model which came along some ten years later have captured a good supply of staunch friends, the original swell fork on a Montana three-quarter tree still holds its own among working cowboys.

But even there we find no set rule to go by among these later cosmopolitanites of American cattledom. True, regional differences have largely disappeared; cowboys West and East are all one. Yet, the proportion of high cantles and pommels runs higher in the Southwest and east of the Rockies. Elaborately carved leather, silver trimmings, and nickel steel horns still flourish more in their old home on the west slope. Simpler styles predominated on the plains, where square skirts and open reins are more often seen. The West still cherishes its heritages of big tapaderos and romal-type bridles.

Likewise, the plains country tends to favor plainer chainless bits, shading off to the popular half-breeds and roller-ports with bit chains as one goes north. The more elaborate creations with rich mountings hold their old leading position west of the Sierras. The same holds true with chaps, headstalls, and all that makes up the cowboy's gear; the place of origin still claims a preponderance of local developments peculiarly suitable to that region or the habitual tastes of the inhabitants.

The Texan's dislike for the Mexican spur chains dragging under the instep led to the invention of upturned heel bands and swinging buttons, which mark the typical boot spurs whose rowels barely touch the ground. They remain the favorite style from Mexico to Canada.

Farther west, the general choice leans toward a modified version of the early Californios' big and highly embellished spurs in fancy designs. Quirts have stayed pretty well within their place of origin, while hackamores still retain their greatest popularity in the West.

At the same time, it is no novelty to see a Dakota puncher wearing Mexican spurs and Colorado chaps, and riding a Montana saddle with Oregon rigging cinched down with a Nevada hair cinch over a gaily striped Hudson's Bay blanket on an Arizona mustang while he upsets an Idaho steer with the Texan's style of tie-down roping. The cowboy is an individualist. Regimentation has never found him to be a peg that would fit into any neatly machined hole. First and last, whatever he outfits himself with is a reflection of his own particular personality. And despite his varied regional characteristics, nonconformity, and independence of thought and action, he remains the only American to reserve his true identity intact through two centuries of economic and social conflict.

About the nearest thing to standardization to be found within his ranks is the boots and hats he wears. When the Southwesterner presented the northwestern buckaroo with a pair of H. J. Justin's newly created cowboy boots during a meeting on the north plains, they both decided that the ultimate had been reached in footwear designed for their trade. Neither has ever found cause to change his mind. Whether now made in Texas, Oregon, the Dakotas, or California, the boots of today's cowboys are essentially the same century-old design that came up the long trail from Texas shortly after 1878.

It is much the same with hats. When John Batterson Stetson brought out his revolutionary concept of an outdoorsman's hat, the "Plainsman," about 1870, he identified for all time the western cowboy with the Stetson trademark. His higher-crowned improvement, with a narrower curled brim, won even greater approval ten years later. Then, along in the late 1890s, the large Carlsbad and Big Four styles came out to meet a still warmer reception. The latter types are still great favorites among the everyday rangemen of the West.

Working cowboys forced to face all weathers in all seasons swear by the high, rounded crowns that furnish a generous air space over the head on hot days and offer no gathering place for rain or snow when it storms. Raw-edged brims that dip slightly toward front and back have always been favored among the majority of cowboys. They have the habit of rolling up the brim while wet, thus setting a permanent half curl in either side. This provides a softer streamlined contour which does not catch the wind like a stiff, flat surface, or get easily knocked askew by ropes, tree limbs, crowding animals, and swinging bunkhouse doors. It also sheds rain better, catches less snow, lends sort of a rakish touch, and looks more like a hat not freshly out of the box.

For some unexplainable reason, the average cowboy never wants his hat to have that just-off-the-shelf appearance. He might sacrifice on luxuries all season, looking forward to the day when he can indulge his desire for a brand-new, thirty-dollar Stetson; then, the moment he gets it in his hands, he'll stomp it into the dust, twist the brim like a dishrag, and knock a few dents in the crown, all so it won't look like something a dude has just bought for his western vacation.

This is not to say that a cowboy does not take pride in his hat. Far from it! He is worse than an old maid at a ribbon counter when it comes to being finicky about the exact features his tastes demand. He will skimp on almost any other item of apparel to buy a particular Stetson that costs perhaps more than his saddle. And he will cherish it as a mother does an only child, even after it has been battered almost beyond recognition.

Nor is this in any sense undeserved sentiment. The durability of Stetson hats is a living legend. Cowcamp sagas all have their quota of "believe it or not" Stetson tales. And there is no dearth of believers. Anyone who has ever wrapped his head in a Stetson for a generous slice of his life knows that the most fantastic yarns may well be true.

For instance, there were the two holdup men whose activities around the Northern Pacific Railroad builders' camp at Weeksville, Montana, in 1882, made them the leading characters in a vigilante hanging. They were buried with their clothes on, including their Stetson hats. When the grave was accidentally uncovered by a grading crew building a highway into nearby Thompson Falls, in 1924, the two skeletons still had their hats with them, both recognizable among the bare bones after their forty-two-year burial.

Another case concerns a forest ranger who was trapped by a forest fire. With no chance to escape the encircling flames, he hurriedly chopped out a narrow trench with his hatchet and covered himself up to the chin with dirt. Then he snugged his Stetson down over his face as a sort of breathing lung. It was truly an unexpected surprise when, rushing in on the heels of the burned-out fire, his companions found him still alive. The hat still held its shape and looked natural, except for being charred coal-black. Although it fell to pieces when they picked it up, it had served its purpose, as Stetsons so invariably do.

This sort of dependability, along with their close association with western outdoorsmen through almost a century, has made the big-style Stetsons virtually synonymous with the West in all languages. So well has this ingrained itself in the public consciousness that there might be more than a little truth in the story of the Montana puncher who picked up the punctured derby hat which had just been shot off of a dude's head. Turning the hat carelessly in his hands, the cowboy happened to notice the Stetson trademark stamped on the sweatband. Turning quickly to his partner, he exclaimed, "Look at that, will yo'! Why, this dang thing is a plumb counterfeit!"

On a par with Stetson's hat, Levi's pants, and Colt's revolver stands Oliver Winchester's rifle in the typical cowboy picture. In the everyday work of the backcountry, it often becomes necessary to pack a rifle. Sick or crippled animals occasionally have to be put out of their misery. Throughout the unpeopled rangelands it is the average cowboy's responsibility to serve as a protector and caretaker for the untended livestock. At any odd moment, he may find a gun to be the only suitable instrument for his needs. Furthermore, most Westerners carry saddle guns when they head out for the tall uncut during hunting season. Thus there is no novelty in a scabbarded carbine appearing as a regular part of any rider's outfit.

Such weapons are ordinarily carried in leather scabbards suspended from the saddle by sling straps. The positions in which they are slung is about the only variation. This actually boils down to four basic methods, two of which are seldom seen among experienced cowmen.

No one of experience would be found guilty of carrying a naked gun hung on the saddle by any sort of sling straps. Allowing the weapon to bang around without protection for the sights and finished stock is a crime against any gun. No less a crime against both man and horse would be the act of exposing trigger

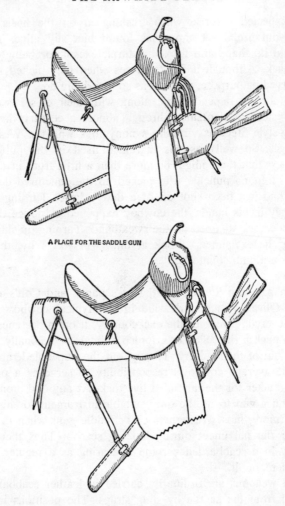

A PLACE FOR THE SADDLE GUN

and hammer assembly to the myriad accidents that might happen on any horseback ride through rough country.

The rifle-carrying method most often encountered is to run the front sling strap through the saddle fork; the back one is held by a loop in the tie strings or, with a double-rigged outfit, the back rigging ring. Properly adjusted, the gun rides under the bend of the knee, with the stock flat against the horse's upper shoulder. The chief disadvantages of this style are that the stock can jab

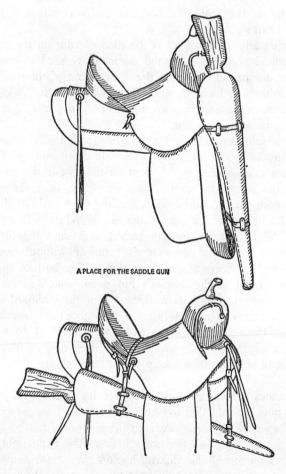

A PLACE FOR THE SADDLE GUN

into the animal's neck on short right-hand turns, and it has a way of hooking a handful of herbage every now and then riding in thick brush.

Slinging the gun at a more acute angle to bring the stock up above the animal's neck makes it still worse about snagging brush, being in the way when roping, handling an unpredictable mount, or doing any of the many things that fall to a rider's lot when in the wilds. Furthermore, such a position puts the muzzle of the gun so low that the horse will often knock it against logs and rocks over which it may be scrambling. This is not only damaging to the scabbard, but can easily result in a bent or broken front sight.

Most unsatisfactory of all is the idea of slinging the scabbard in a vertical position, a method occasionally used in early days by a few uninitiated visitors to the West. Some greenhorns may be found using this method, until they learn better. Awkward to draw from, and usually in the way of everything else, it is chiefly noted for its nuisance value.

Diametrically opposite is the very neat and handy arrangement of turning both gun and scabbard upside down and end for end. One sling strap fastens to the front tie strings and the other goes around the base of the cantle. Run through a slit in the opposite jockey string and anchored down flat, the strap will not climb the cantle or be noticeable under the rider. When correctly positioned under the knee, the gun muzzle will slant slightly downward to fit in behind the horse's shoulder without being low enough to interfere with leg movements. The butt of the stock drops in ahead of the animal's hip bone, which serves as an added safeguard against its working out of the scabbard in steep uphill scrambles. There is little to fear about its working out, however. The inside of the scabbard, tapering as it does toward the lower edge, allows the gun to wedge itself downward and acts as a sort of self-adjusting clamp under the pressure of the rider's leg.

Advocates of this style claim a security equal to any of the others, plus the fact that the gun and scabbard are never in the way. They also deny any brush-catching propensities by the slim muzzle flattened against the horse's body. The front sight, riding as it does on top of the muzzle, has no chance for contact with dangerous objects. The backward-turned stock sheds any entanglements and rests low enough to offer no obstruction to any action of the rider. Altogether, those who use this method swear by it on all counts.

In use while mounted, it offers a facility equal, if not superior, to any other style. A single straight pull with one backward sweep of the hand puts the gun in immediate position for action. For ground shooting, the rider grasps the stock as his leg swings over the horse's rump, bringing the weapon with him as he drops to the ground, stock against his shoulder and barrel grip ready to his left hand, all in one single fluid, movement. For quick shooting without lost motion, it easily surpasses having to pull the gun forward and then reverse it before starting to dismount. A reversed movement puts it back in the scabbard with equal dispatch.

But whichever way he chooses to carry it, the handy little carbine is, like all other items of his outfit, a practical adjunct proven by time and trial to serve one of the many special needs of the American cowboy.

## Chapter XI

## HIDES, HORNS, BEEF AND BRAINS

Cholla Ellis pulled his horse up short at the bend in the canyon. The blat of a calf jerked his eyes to the chaparral clump banking the base of the ten-foot cut-bank a dozen rods ahead. He only half heard the sharp rattle of stones above and to the right as the old longhorn cow shot over the top of the sheer bank, eyes bulging in fury and the coarse hair on her lined back standing on end. She came down like a piledriver, all four feet bunched as she hit the chaparral.

The brush was still cracking as she rebounded skyward to swing half around and again drive both front feet at something hidden in the thicket. Cholla's tense face relaxed in a wide grin as the squalling fur-bundle of mountain lion catapulted into the open, dragging one hind leg. The next moment it had three-cornered itself into a jumble of boulders across the canyon.

At the same time, the week-old, brockle-faced calf showed itself from under the lee of the bank, bloody claw marks streaking its light-colored rump. The cow lunged through the brush in pursuit of the lion, still snorting death and destruction. Halfway to the boulders, she lurched to a stop, swinging her head in answer to the calf's plaintive bleat. Cholla's grin broadened as he turned his horse back down the canyon. He couldn't see as he was needed around there.

As a matter of fact, the old Texas longhorn seldom needed anybody's help. If self-sufficiency didn't start with him, he was at least a charter member in the lodge. When the chips were down, he usually delivered; if not by force, then by wit, cunning, or plain old indomitable guts.

Here was a creature whose personality somewhat resembled that of his two-legged contemporary, the old-time Texan. Not always conventional in appearance and often inclined to eccentricity in action, his was the kind of character which spawned legends and wrote history. Like the cowboy, the Indian, and the frontier marshal, he stands even today as a symbol of that western wilderness which became an empire. Without him, old-time cowmen are fond of saying, Chicago and Kansas City would never have been built or the arid sections of the West settled.

But that was a long time ago. Mention of the longhorn in this shopping-center age usually brings to mind a visionary caricature of scrawny hide stretched over an angular, bony frame, the whole serving as sort of a kitelike tail to a pair of fantastically long horns. What little meat might be secreted underneath the nondescript hide is dismissed as something akin to a slab of cardboard or a weather-seasoned boot top.

Such opinions, unfortunately, do a great injustice to the old longhorns. They did make good beef and plenty of it. It was the length of time it took them to make it that worked against them and contributed so heavily to their demise.

In contrast to the quick growth of modern, improved cattle, longhorns did not mature until they were four or five years old. Moreover, they did not reach their maximum weight of twelve to eighteen hundred pounds until the age of eight or ten years. On maturity, however, they took on suitable fat and furnished beef quite comparable to any other cattle. Most of the old-timers argue that longhorn meat was even richer than any beef available in later years. What was more important, longhorns would fatten under conditions that would send most of today's breeds to the canner's block.

Too, their sagacity, toughness, and ability to take care of themselves under any circumstances placed them in a class all their own. Few of the world's cattle could have survived the rigors of the Southwest in the early 1800s, much less gone on to develop a strain capable of populating the entire West. Predators, storms, and searing droughts all no doubt claimed their toll, but the longhorns took such obstacles in their stride as their numbers increased to over six million in Texas by 1865. That was a shining example of their durability and brains, considering the conditions under which they thrived. If the longhorn couldn't whip an adversary, he had what it took to make a believer out of him otherwise.

That dean of western raconteurs, J. Frank Dobie, tells of one such animal that ranged over in New Mexico. He was a red bull about six years old. A couple of cowboys came across him out on the range one day. Previous associations, not always soothing to cowboy temperament, had made both well acquainted with the critter. As they now rode up on him, they saw that he had one eye gone and a big chunk of hide hanging down from his back just behind the shoulders. His foreparts had been badly clawed, while his horns were covered with freshly dried blood. The injuries were comparatively fresh. Everything indicated a recent encounter of considerable interest.

The men started quartering the vicinity for further enlightenment. They found it a few minutes later. A half acre of shin oak had been uprooted and smashed into kindling on a little bench around a bend in the canyon. The place looked like someone had tackled it with a bull-tongue plow. And there, draped across a downed log, they found the carcass of a dead grizzly bear. The beast's entrails were strung out across the ground and its hair was matted with dried blood. The bull made a complete recovery.

Another bull of similar disposition claimed the unique distinction of having been the only cow-brute ever to rout an army. That was in 1847, when General Zachary Taylor was marching his force from Corpus Christi, Texas, to the lower Rio Grande. It was a big and open country. The bull had, for reasons of his own, selected this quiet solitude as a private retreat. The sudden noisy invasion of marching soldiers apparently struck him as an outright attack on property rights. Then, to heap insult on injury, one of the soldiers shot at him as he voiced his objections through a cloud of freshly pawed dust.

Unfortunately, the soldier was a poor marksman. The next instant, the bull ended the discussion by plunging headlong into the ranks, scattering men right and left. Afraid to shoot for fear of hitting dodging comrades, and perhaps too busy with their feet to have much time to use their hands, the demoralized army slowly recovered its poise to see the animal wring its tail in derision as it lumbered away. The entire Mexican Army was unable to duplicate this feat later at Monterey.

Creatures of such nature do not sidestep difficulties; they surmount them. For the longhorns, this was an honest heritage. Their ancestors were the fierce and crafty brutes Don Gregorio de Villalobos had brought to Mexico in 1521. Villalobos needed something as tough as the country he was trying to settle. He made a good choice. The sharp-horned, indomitable Andalusians not only put him in the cattle business, but went on to stock most of the ranches that were soon to spread all over the face of western America.

In a letter written in 1555 by Robert Tomson, an English trader who had done considerable trafficking with New Spain during its early years, we find mention of that country's great numbers of "Spanish cattell which dayly do increase and are of greater growth than ours." He goes on to tell of one ranchero who owned twenty thousand head at that time, only thirty-five years after the first cattle had landed at Vera Cruz.

Later brought north to the Rio Grande territory, great numbers of these animals went AWOL in the brush country of southeast Texas. There the first American settlers found them, crafty as lobo wolves and dangerous as Comanches, roaming at will in a country that so well complemented their savage dispositions.

The new immigrants from Missouri, Kentucky, and Tennessee brought a smattering of eastern cattle with them from their homeland, as pioneers ever had the habit of doing. Turned out to graze on the unfenced range, these animals crossed with the wild, black Andalusians during the ensuing years. In the course of time, the latter faded out of the picture to leave the multicolored longhorns. The Indians called this new strain "rainbow cattle," a name which saw considerable use among the white cowmen of later years.

Their great diversity of color, another distinctive longhorn characteristic, made the name well founded. No other breed claimed such a wide variation of coats. While reds and browns predominated, these shaded off all the way from black to yellow. And, as an enlivening touch, there was always a generous admixture of roans, brindles, whites, duns, buckskins, line-backs, and all imaginable combinations of spots, paints, pintos, and speckles.

Environment and living conditions of a harsh land bred into the longhorns all the qualities needed for survival. They would fight like cougars, run like antelope, and swim like seals. Shanghai Pierce, down on the Texas coast, in fact, had the habit of speaking of his cattle as the "sea lions." Anyway, they acknowledged no superiors, when it came to taking care of themselves.

Perennial scarcity of feed and water taught them to live under what often were almost impossible conditions. Droughts frequently compelled them to range far from any watering place in search of the scanty feed. This often would necessitate a ten- to twenty-mile hike for a drink; the longhorns would make the trip only every other day. Old-time cattlemen agree that it was not uncommon, at such times, to see one or two cows take over the care of the entire calf herd while the rest of the adult cattle went to water. Only when the latter returned would the babysitting cows leave their charges to head out for their own delayed refreshments.

The African lion is said to be the only other animal known to display such a practice. This would probably confirm the old Texan's assertion that his longhorns had picked up a little lion blood somewhere along the line.

On occasions, when the only feed was a prohibitive distance from water, these cattle might go for almost unbelievable periods with the succulent cactus as their only source of moisture.

During one extended drought in west Texas, a well-known rancher missed one of his big steers. As all his cattle were bone poor, and the range was practically denuded, he concluded that the beast had crawled off and given up the ghost. Several weeks later, however, he happened to come upon the animal some twenty-five miles from the home ranch. And the steer was rolling fat. This was in Spanish-dagger country and the plants were in bloom. All the moisture the critter had been getting was from the dagger flowers. The man took him home and butchered him. Upon dressing the carcass out, he found the animal's bladder shrunk up to the size of a goose egg. Otherwise, the steer was normal.

Andy Adams wrote about one desert trail drive in the 1880s,

during which the herd traveled a waterless stretch for five or six days. The lowing of the brutes became pitiful in the final stages, and some of them went blind, but the herd kept in motion until a stream finally was reached. There, unlike other cattle, who would have drunk themselves to death, the longhorns simply stood in the deeper water all night, drinking very little. Their intelligence paid off in that the entire herd recovered from the ordeal.

These longhorn herds also had the unique ability to put on weight and fatten themselves as they grazed their way across the prairies at ten to fifteen miles a day, crossing deserts and swimming streams on the way. Several herds are known to have swum the Mississippi River at various points between Vicksburg and Baton Rouge. It all served to demonstrate that the longhorn held the answer to his own transportation problem.

In the brush country of southeast Texas it was often necessary to rope the wild cimarrones, or outlaws, of the thorn thickets individually and tie them up until additional help or a tame ox could be brought to escort the captive away. During one such roundup, shortly after the Civil War, one of the cowboys roped a maverick bull and tied him in a thicket until the day's catch could be collected. For some unknown reason, this particular animal was overlooked when the others were taken to the ranch. Twenty-one days later, the ranch owner found the bull still tied in the thicket. It was still on its feet and still fighting to get loose.

As might be expected of such salty characters, this toughness was not confined to animals in the prime of life. Age only added to their hardiness and cunning, while the calves were as lusty as their buffalo neighbors in being up and doing for themselves almost as soon as they were dry after birth. Also like the buffalo, a longhorn calf would spring from a supine position to its feet with a single move.

One of the most extraordinary longhorn treks in history was that of old Sancho. This black-and-white steer was adopted by the Mexican wife of a Frio County Texan, when its mother was found dead. Señora Kerr was a childless woman who found her outlet for affections in caring for pets. She proceeded to mother the orphaned calf with the help of an impressed wild cow. During the process, she formed the habit of slipping the calf tidbits of corn, tamales, and other pepper-seasoned foods. Sancho developed quite a liking for the dainties. Thoughts of mealtime always prevented him from straying far from home. Night would invariably find him returning to the ranch for a possible hand-out and his chosen bedground under a certain mesquite tree outside the gate.

When he was a three-year-old, Kerr sold him, over his wife's protests, to some neighbors named Shiner, who were trailing three herds north to Wyoming that spring. The new owners road branded Sancho with their 7Z and started him off with the first herd. But Sancho didn't think much of the idea. He continually kept trying to break back. After ten days on the trail, he made his escape. The second herd met him headed homeward, his thoughts no doubt on corn and chili peppers. This crew threw him in with their herd and took him along. During a stampede shortly afterward, the steer again disappeared. But it was three times and out for Sancho. The third Shiner herd intercepted his southward course. They managed to keep him pointed toward the North Star until they reached the Bighorn country of Wyoming. There the new owners branded him CR and turned him out on the range.

But Sancho's heart was true to his tamales. Early spring found him arising from under his favorite tree one morning to greet his astonished mistress. He was still wearing his road brand and the Wyoming CR. The two thousand lonely mid-winter miles had worked no apparent ill effects on the animal. Kerr said he was in first-class condition, except for his hoofs being worn down. Such a love for the homeland appealed to the Texas spirit. Sancho was allowed to live out his life within reach of his chili basin and mesquite shade.

It is to be hoped that fate did not cheat him of a full lifetime, which not uncommonly ran to twenty-five or thirty years with this breed. Old Geronimo, that famous Texas steer who had been an outlaw most of his life and wore the brands of six different own-ers, was reported to have been over thirty-six years old when he died.

When fully grown, their height corresponded well with their extraordinary life span. Longhorns often grew to sixteen or seven-teen hands tall during their lifetime (a "hand" is the equivalent of four inches). There is record of a steer in Live Oak County,

Texas, which, standing normally, measured eight feet from his hoofs to the top of his horns. His horns, which curved upward, measured seven feet nine inches from tip to tip, or approximately nine feet by following the curves.

Such horns, however, were unusual. Five- to six-foot spreads were fairly common, but longer than that were considered exceptional. The frequently heard accounts of twelve- to eighteen-foot spreads are somewhat akin to stories of the hoop snake and Rocky Mountain hodag: it is always something someone has heard about from somebody else, but never actually seen. A set of horns with a nine-foot spread, from the Texas coast, was presented to President Grant, and there is said to have been two pairs of similar length at the 1893 exposition in Chicago. Eight- to eight-and-a-half-foot spreads were encountered occasionally at rare intervals.

These exceptionally big spreads were the product of the older animals; a longhorn's horns kept on growing until he was twelve or fifteen years old. They started growing wrinkles out from the base at the age of three. The well-wrinkled horn bases of big steers were pretty good age calendars, winning them the title of "old mossy horns."

But the most peculiar feature about these extraordinary horns was the fact that the extremely long ones were found only on steers. Bull and cow horns were overlarge, by cow-brute standards, but they never developed the fantastic shapes and excessive lengths of those grown by steers. Moreover, the longer horns were usually found on steers raised in the wetter, warmer sections down toward the gulf. Colder and drier climates seemed to have a discouraging effect on horn growth.

But regardless of what they wore on their heads, it was what the longhorns carried under their hides that lifted Texas from financial prostration to leadership in the cattle industry. Of course, this didn't materialize all at once. Big events seldom do. And the longhorn was ever one to need time to fulfill his destiny.

It was shortly after the War Between the States that this destiny waved a beckoning hand against the northern horizon. The opening of the great northern-plains territory had suddenly captured the attention of all prospective cowmen. And the first requirement of ranching is cattle. That was when the eyes of the world first began turning toward Texas. The long-horned herds below the Brazos were the answer to the Northerner's prayer. Likewise, the Northerner's purse was God's answer to impoverished Texas.

As these countless herds pounded out their dusty trails over half a continent, it was only natural that various characters among such rugged individualists should command special attention. Cow-camp annals are crowded with legendary longhorns whose wit or courage won them a place in history.

One such animal was Old Blue. Charles Goodnight bought him in 1874, when he was a four-year-old. Goodnight was making up a herd to take to his Colorado ranch near Pueblo, and Old Blue immediately elected himself leader of the bunch. The way he kept his position throughout the journey won the greatest approval from his new owner. Good lead steers were rare and highly prized animals. When Goodnight moved back to Texas, it was Old Blue who broke trail for the herd. Later, he led most of the Goodnight trail herds to the railroad at Dodge City, Kansas, sometimes going twice a year.

During this latter period, they put a new brass bell with a shiny collar on him. Old Blue displayed as much pride in the accouterment as a kid with a new concho belt. Too, he recognized the dignity of his position to a greater extent when equipped with this new badge of office. After leading the herd all day, he would go off and bed down by himself in haughty aloofness. At day-break, his solitary figure would circle the herd, then move au-thoritatively toward the trail. On the return journey, he took his place with the saddle-horse remuda, often traveling up to thirty miles a day without lagging. He served faithfully in his chosen profession until his death in 1890.

Bill Blocker, another famous trail driver, had a big bay steer with black spots which was of similar disposition. This animal also created his own place as a leader and never relinquished it. He became as proud as a peacock and as independent as a hog on ice. Blocker made a practice of riding alongside him with one hand on the steer's horn. Together, it was said, they could take a herd through anything.

But not all of these fabled celebrities chose to walk to glory in the service of man. They, like the individuals who handled them, were a tough, free-spirited breed. Regimentation and oppressive authority were doctrines which generated no warmth in their hearts. From the longhorn's point of view, this was a free country, leaving one's destiny in his own hands. And he had a way of practicing his belief.

Frank S. Hastings gives a good example of this in his *Recollections of a Ranchman*. The steer in question was among a bunch of old mossy horns at a packing plant in Leavenworth, Kansas. As the beast passed down the slaughter chute, the killer struck him a stunning blow between the eyes. The steer dropped instantly. He was immediately dropped through the trapdoor and dragged to the skinning bed. There, at the first touch of the knife against his throat, he leaped to his feet in a single bound, shedding skinners like chaff. At the same moment, he spied daylight through an open door at the rear of the building. Without a pause, he catapulted through the door, jumped a story and a half to the ground, and then swam the Missouri River to a sandbar a quarter mile distant. There he shook himself, bawled his distaste for all such foolishness, cocked his tail in the air, and disappeared into the distance.

Another time, a herd was being shoved into a hide-and-tallow plant at Fulton, Texas. Midway in the proceedings, a big brindle steer suddenly broke away from the bunch and, eluding pursuit, plunged into the sea. He swam twelve miles across the bay to a point at Lemar and made his escape.

Then there was a self-emancipated freethinker up in Idaho. This was a spotted bull born of a southern longhorn cow. The cow took him to the tall uncut shortly after he was born, presumably for instruction in the rights of personal liberty. There, the two ranged alone, seen occasionally but eluding all roundups for years. The cow finally disappeared, but her son held down the old homestead until some cowboys were detailed to bring him in. He was then ten years old.

The men managed to rout him out and get him in with a herd headed for market, but he was as spooky as a bull elk in a cornfield. The second night on the trail, he made his escape during a storm and threatened stampede. He then ran free until another organized hunt was made for him, two years later. This party was chasing him, after a hard but successful search, when a big bear suddenly rose in front of the bull. The critter never swerved. He hit the bear head on, bowled the beast over, and kept going. However, he was eventually caught, tied to a tame ox, and thrown in with a beef herd.

But the longhorn still kept faith with his mother's teachings. The trouble he caused in the herd was a story in itself, not to mention the misery he dealt the ox to which he was tied. The third night on the trail, the herd broke in a stampede. One rider, chasing the runaways, caught the stifled bawl of a critter in distress. Investigation disclosed the outlaw and the tame ox wound up tight around a tree which they had run straddle of. The wheezing ox was already nearly choked to death. To save its life, the puncher cut the rope. That was all the longhorn needed. He was gone in a flash. Everyone concerned, if not secretly glad to have him gone, respected his dedication to freedom enough that he was allowed to go his lonely, unreconstructed way, until he disappeared for good a few years later.

Cowboys, as a rule, are prone to appreciate the outstanding characteristics of their four-footed charges. Pride, intelligence, courage, independence, and defiance in individual animals has a way of striking a responsive chord in the minds of rangemen. It might almost be called a meeting of kindred spirits. Even the misfits and clowns of the animal world are often raised to legendary heights by such uninhibited souls reminiscing over a campfire.

Thus it is that the epic of Old Brindle has become a classic of the southwestern ranges. While raconteurs may possibly deal a little loosely with the truth on a few points, men long familiar with the old longhorns hesitate to cite any falsities in the story. Instead, they are prone to lapse into memories of other animals equally clever in certain respects.

This particular ox was a member of Joe Goodbread's freight outfit. On one notable occasion, he was yoked up with his teammates for a trip out to the railroad for a load of freight. All the wagons in the outfit had trailers, each of which bore the customary canvas cover, open in front and closed with a puckering string behind. The company camped nights along the trail, turning the oxen out on the range to feed. When Old Brindle, already famous for his sly craftiness, was not to be found with the herd one morning, everyone simply concluded that he had taken French leave and gone home. As there was no use in going after him at that late date, the party yoked up one of the spare oxen in his place and went on.

Half a day later and some eight miles farther along the trail, the outfit camped for dinner. During the course of the meal, Goodbread remarked that his wagon would have to be greased. He said it had been pulling like a stoneboat all morning.

When he walked around the wagon to get his grease bucket, some minutes later, he happened to glance into the open end of the trail wagon. The yell he let out echoed across the prairie like the blast of a cannon. Everyone snapped to attention instantly, following Joe's pointing finger. There in the wagon, hidden by the canvas cover, they saw the missing Brindle stretched out and sleeping like the village disgrace on Sunday morning. Whether or not he was using Joe's bedroll for a pillow is still an unsettled question. But there was no argument over the fact that, instead of being angry at the trick played on him, Goodbread fairly bloated with pride over his ox's smartness. The ox, witnesses of the event later declared, was equally proud of himself as he yawned deliberately and jumped to the ground.

Other longhorns were of comparable or greater distinction. Bunkhouse legends will always hold their quota of such outstanding individualists. But the longhorn himself, like the most of the other great figures who shaped the course of history, was forced into oblivion under the wheels of progress. Fenced ranges and the demand for quick beef reduced him to a tradition in less time than it took the railroad and the settler to do the same thing to the Indian and the buffalo.

When an attempt was made to preserve for posterity a remnant of the unique breed at Oklahoma's Wichita Wild Life Preserve, in 1927, an extensive search of Texas produced only twenty cows and three bulls of the true strain. But they are a virile species. At present, with the help of a few interested breeders in the Southwest, their progeny are a fair way toward perpetuating the memory of the American cattleland's rugged birth.

This would be especially true if they should happen to emulate the herd of a certain questionable character out in west Texas. When forced to explain the phenomenal increase of his herd, the man claimed it was due to his steers bringing home stray calves every now and then.

"Them steers," he said, "just seem to have a plumb unreasonable honin' for youngsters. Where they get the little fellers, I don't know; but bein' longhorns, there ain't much a man c'n do about it."

*Chapter XII*


## THE HORSE THAT WON THE WEST


While the longhorn was busy living up to his ancient heritage
the mustang horse was equally busy keeping pace with the cowboy
in an effort to establish similar support for the cowcountry. Built
from the choicest materials selected from six thousand years of
stockraising, these three foundation columns rose straight and true
against the western sky. And although designed by centuries of
cumulative skills, each was distinctly American and unique unto
itself. By the same token, the separate singularities of these three
great pillars of western development have always moved side by
side in parallel courses.

Fully as exceptional in his own ways as the cowboy or the
longhorn, the mustang of the Southwest was an animal without any
exact counterpart in the known horse world. Although faulty in
some respects, he stood for over two and a half centuries as the
greatest natural ally of man, both red and white, throughout the
West. He alone turned the somewhat ineffectual Indian nations
into what General Crook once termed the best light cavalry forces
the world ever knew, and made it possible for them to hold the
bulk of their native land against overwhelming invaders for the
best part of a century. Without the mustang, western exploration
would have been retarded for untold years. But for him, those
intrepid mountain-men would never have been able to penetrate
every hidden corner of the West and establish their fabulous fur
industry in the short space of twenty years. Then, again, it was

this animal which pulled the stages and carried the mail over half a continent; built the railroad grades for expanding commerce and turned the homesteader's furrow; carried religion, law, and education to the frontier settlements; hauled the goods of an empire in the making, and bore the burden of cattledom's magical development. In short, it is not too much to say that all that vast region of inestimable wealth lying between the Mississippi and the Pacific owes its very being to the strength, spirit, and endurance of the mustang horse.

This great territory might do well to forget for a moment its gasoline fumes, clanking caterpillar treads, and shrieking automobile horns and take time out to erect a fitting monument—something in the nature of the *Christ of the Andes,* only of a more imposing appearance, set atop the Rocky Mountains—in honor of this patron saint of western progress which was slaughtered on the altar of cheap dog feed.

The mustang, as we have seen, owes its parentage to the Arabbarb horses bred in Spain and brought to America by the conquistadores. But from there on he became an individual in his own right, as purely American as human descendants of ancestors contemporary with his own. Perhaps he was nature's actual restoration of the ancient American horse. This continent possesses qualities which automatically develop characteristics unique in the animal world, as it does among the human race. It is a moot question. But the fact remains that this animal will ever stand in the annals of pioneer history head-high and shoulder to shoulder with the nation's great personalities in exploration, building, and development.

From the very start of Spanish occupation, these animals began their phenomenal spread across the Western Hemisphere. Much of this was forwarded by Indian interest in the wonder creatures. Much more was instituted by the animals themselves. It was a big country. Early settlements were only pinpricks in the immensity of wilderness. Lost, strayed, or stolen stock had to travel only short distances to lose all touch with domesticity. Blessed as they were with a high grade of intelligence, horses that found themselves separated from restrictive influences soon succumbed to the charm of the wild, untrammeled freedom. There, thanks to the lush forage, kindly climate, and freedom from enemies prevalent in the

West, they waxed fat and multiplied in unbelievable numbers. Fanning out to the north and east from the settlements scattered along the Rio Grande, they spread across the short-grass plains to meet the dawn of the eighteenth century as one of the country's leading animal entities.

Generally speaking, this movement coincided fairly well with the spread of horse culture among the Indians, already dealt with in Chapter IV. In many particularly favorable sections, however, the wild herds far exceeded those controlled by the redmen.

When Americans first began filtering into the little-known Louisiana Territory, they found the prolific mustangs there in astonishing number. Some authorities place the figure as high as two million by 1800. In the light of regional accounts left us by competent observers of that period, such overall estimates would seem to be safely on the conservative side.

After crossing the Texas plains in 1846, Lieutenant Ulysses S. Grant wrote: ". . . Bands of wild horses extended as far as the eye could reach; there was no estimating their numbers." A contemporary traveler in the same region noted: ". . . The trampling of their hoofs sounded like the roar of the surf on a rocky beach." Many other settlers and travelers in Texas and New Mexico wrote of their impressions in a similar vein.

Much the same pattern existed in the North, although on a smaller scale. Untended horses thrived better and increased faster where there was less snow and milder winters. Natural instinct tended to concentrate the majority of the wild ones in the more equitable regions of the Southwest.

When the ranchmen, town builders, and transportation agents began moving into the country, they viewed the wild mustangs as a source of supply for necessary stock. Many men took up the occupation of trapping or running down the ownerless animals for sale to ready purchasers. The Comanches had long practiced this craft, trading their captives to poorer-supplied neighbors for desirable commodities. Mexican vaqueros, too, were especially adapted to such work. Later, not a few cowboys found it an exciting and often profitable business well up into the twentieth century.

Men who hunted mustangs for profit were commonly called mustangers. The name "mustanger" is an English word derived from the Spanish *mesteno,* which in turn comes from *mesta,* the Spanish name for a collective group of stockraisers. The suffix *eno* means "belonging to." Thus, horses which had escaped from their owners to run wild were designated *mestenos.* A person who worked at catching such animals for himself or the rightful owners was naturally known as a *mestenero.* American tongues soon twisted these words into "mustang" and "mustanger," broadening their scope to include all Spanish horses and any hunter of the wild stock.

On the northern ranges, "bronco," or "bronc," was used in preference to "mustang" in most sections as far south as Oklahoma. "Bronco" is also a Spanish word, meaning "harsh," "rough," or "wild." It appears to have come into use through the fact that by the time white men began meeting the wild herds in the North, they were no longer considered escaped property; as simply "the wild ones," the name "bronco" was a better appellation. And most of them in their natural state had all the characteristics that the name implies.

Out in the Northwest, the same animal was known as a cayuse. "Cayuse" came from the Indian nation of that name which inhabited eastern Oregon. The Cayuses were famous horsemen whose homeland was overflowing with horses. As their territory straddled most of the length of the old Oregon Trail through the intermountain region, early travelers of that route soon fell into the habit of calling all Indian stock "Cayuse ponies." The inevitable result was a shortening to the single word "cayuses." Later arrivals picked up the name as a common designation for all common or poorer-grade saddle horses throughout the Northwest.

Hunting mustangs became such a good business at one time that the government began holding out the old greedy palm for its rake-off. Mexico passed a law in 1827 that demanded a special license for the right to capture wild horses in Coahuila and Texas. The license called for the payment of two *reals* for each mustang caught, along with two *pesos* for a mule and two reals for a cowbrute. Hunting was permitted only during the open season of October 1 to February 28. Texas enacted similar laws in 1852, 1854, and 1856, covering the territory west of the San Antonio River.

But with growing settlements and increasing need for grass, Texas cattlemen began turning a cold eye toward protection for the mustangs. The year 1858 saw all such laws repealed and a free hand given to anyone with mustanger ambitions. All through this period and on toward the end of the century, much of the foundation stock for the country's needs came from the wild herds.

Even with increasing inroads on their numbers, the wild mustangs held out in imposing strength in many sections. Frank Collinson wrote in the 1870s that fifty thousand was a low estimate of the number still ranging on the Staked Plains at that time. John Young, of south Texas, stated that it was no novelty to see as many as a thousand head in view at one time between the Nueces River and the Rio Grande during the same period.

Countless bands of smaller size took up residence in scattered localities all over the West. Many of these, augmented by ponies of dismounted agency Indians and strayed settler stock, grew to impressive proportions in later years. Additional reinforcements came from the million or more mustangs brought north with the Texas trail herds during the 1868–98 era. And wherever they might be, their numbers helped furnish mounts and harness animals for men with strong nerves and long ropes.

Now, there is a common misconception that animals denied the almighty guiding hand of civilized man will quickly deteriorate and revert to inferior quality. There is some truth in this idea when it comes to domestic creatures, even most breeds of horses. But the mustang was in a class by himself in this respect. Like the buffalo, elk, and deer, he was quite capable of preserving his heritage without the aid of omnipotent supervision.

His was a harsh environment in most cases. Denied comfortable shelter, stored feed, and protection from lurking enemies, he was ever at the mercy of storm, flood, drought, snow, cold, bitter blizzards, and range-parching heat. An occasional panther, bear, or lobo wolf added to his hazards, especially among the young. It was a land where only the fittest survived. The cripples, the weaklings, and the unfit fell by the wayside before they had a chance to propagate their kind. Furthermore, only the stronger and swifter studs were able to capture and retain harems. Second-rate stallions were either killed off by sturdier antagonists or relegated to a bachelor existence. The net result was a mating of the best and the best, from which only the best survived to carry on.

Neither was the mustang addicted to inbreeding. In contrast to other breeds of horses, old-time observers all agree that the wild studs invariably drove their young sons and daughters from the herd before they reached their second year. The fillies would be collected by a herdless sire, usually an older but otherwise sound and sagacious animal, who had been deposed from command of his older mares by a particularly strong youngster.

As all stockmen know, this breeding of young to old is a sound practice for herd benefits. Some stallions even went so far in selective breeding as to admit mares of only a certain color into their bands.

The whole proceeding worked toward improved speed, strength, and stamina, rather than any deterioration. Few men who knew them will disagree with the statement that the true mustang developed himself into the toughest and most durable piece of horseflesh this continent has ever seen. Catlike in agility, surefooted as mountain goats, and possessing an inbred instinct for danger, they were unequaled as wilderness mounts. Some were of good size, a few being superb animals; but most were on the small side, running from 600 up to around 800 pounds. They never knew the taste of grain or any forage other than what they could gather on the open range. Yet it was nothing unusual for one of them to carry a 160-pound man and a 40-pound saddle all day at a steady lope. They could go longer without feed and farther between waterings than anything outside the Arabian desert. In canny wisdom, craft, and the ability to take care of themselves under any and all conditions, they stood in a class that no modern horse can duplicate. Quite comparable to the old-time mountain-men in individuality and self-sufficiency, they neither needed nor wanted any of the refinements that went with the circumscribed life of their softer and more sheltered cousins.

There were many fabulous stories, still recurrent in the West, about the individualism and indomitability of certain mustangs who paid homage to no man. The spirit, wit, and physical effort they exhibited in eluding the ensnaring coils of the welfare state might well be an object lesson to many humans.

There was, for instance, the Ghost of the Staked Plains. He

was a milk-white stud who melted as if by magic into a cloud of vanishing dust upon the approach of any mounted riders. Seen occasionally on a lonely hilltop, his silken mane and tail rippling in the wind as he guarded his chosen band of mares, or glimpsed cautiously approaching a scentless waterhole, he would promptly fade into the landscape on a rush of flying hoofs at hint of any untoward movement. He thus remained the master of his own destiny through the 1870s and into the 1880s.

It was in March 1882 that a pair of buffalo hunters set out to emancipate him from his uncared-for existence. After carefully stationing relays of first-class mounts at intervals about his range, one of the men took up the Ghost's trail and gave chase. Alternating with a fresh mount and rider as each relay station was neared, the two hunters ran the stud for four days, covering a distance of three hundred miles. He was still going strong when they cornered him at last in the angle of a desert sink. The Ghost saw his danger too late. All escape cut off, he screamed his defiance at the men, whirled on his hind feet, and plunged bodily into the sink. A few lunging, deliberate steps took him without deviation into the deepest of the quagmire before the enemy could get a rope on him. There, with the wild glare of uncompromise in his eyes, he swiftly sank from sight.

Another stallion with similar intentions and determination was successfully roped when he first plunged into his boggy route to destruction. His captors managed to snake him out alive, but to no avail. There, at the end of his rope, he simply refused all feed and water until he died of starvation.

More successful was the steel-blue stud with silver mane and tail that ranged the intermountain region of the Northwest in the 1880s. A quartet of experienced mustangers once managed to get him into a trap corral, but there their luck ran out. He fought all four of them to a standstill, then crashed his way over the high pole fence and took off for parts unknown.

Unlike most horses, which usually return to their home range, the big blue quit the country for good. He apparently traveled by night, hiding out in the daytime, until he eventually turned up in the Montana badlands. There he was seen occasionally in widely separated localities, nearly always by moonlight. Although he finally disappeared entirely, presumably by death or accident, his was the spirit and intelligence which preserves freedom and the chosen way of life to the end.

A similar individualistic outlook was enjoyed by a Six Up and Down mustang from Texas. His owners, the Newman Cattle Company, had a ranch in the Davis Mountains of that state and another in Montana. This particular horse was included in a bunch of saddle stock taken from Texas to the Montana ranch the spring of 1891. Arriving at his new home late that season, he was turned out on the range with the rest of his companions for the winter. Just when he disappeared is uncertain, but he was nowhere to be found when spring roundup rolled around. However, some eighteen months later, in the fall of 1893, he drifted in to the home ranch in Texas, none the worse for his long, lonesome journey. The Newmans thought that kind of home-loving affection deserved consideration. He was, in consequence, allowed to serve out his days in the land of his choice.

Mustang sagas of this nature could go on endlessly. Every section of the West has its quota. They all depict the unique qualities which made the animal such an admirable character in the eyes of a horseman. Although the average Westerner has an incurable habit of putting a small fact through the paces of a spinning rope until the loop stretches out to fantastic size, there is plenty of existing proof that he regards the little Spanish horses, like he does his women, more as objects of respect than something for imaginative loquacity.

Some legendary feats of strength and endurance performed by this breed are discussed in Chapter XIV.

Most old-time rangemen hang on to the idea that the bucking habit of western horses is a trait originated by the wild mustangs in ridding themselves of attacking cougars. It is a plausible assumption. The big cats are wont to lie on overhanging limbs or ledges, waiting for the chance to leap onto prey passing beneath them. Such assaults are murderously effective against deer and other grazing animals addicted to blind, heedless flight. It is believed, however, that time and experience taught the more intelligent mustang that his best defense was to come unwound and turn himself wrong side out the instant he felt something on his back. Such violent and concentrated action would be the surest way to put the cat on the ground, where savagely striking hoofs could turn the advantage in the right direction. It is not at all inconceivable that such gyrations as this equine hellion can perform would accomplish that purpose. And many pioneer stockmen left written records of mustangs found with claw scars on their backs, withers, and necks.

Everything considered, this is the most reasonable explanation of why the mustang, alone among all the world's horses, should have such a singular characteristic as the bucking habit. We know it never appeared anywhere else in equine history. Xenophone wrote copiously about the horses of antiquity, going to considerable length in describing all phases of riding, breaking, and training the animals. His dissertations on the various breeds, their habits and propensities, are most complete. Yet, nowhere did he make any mention of a trait faintly resembling the bucking of our western steeds. Other writers through the centuries have given us assorted works on all the various branches and periods of the subject. Historians, explorers, and soldiers also have ever been wont to dwell on the mounts which meant so much to any campaign in the old world. While we do find frequent references to mean horses throughout Asia, Europe, and Africa—horses that bit, struck, kicked, threw themselves, ran away, and the like—there is never a single mention of the spectacular art of bogging the head, throwing a hump in the back, and coming unhinged in the kind of convolutions we know as bucking or pitching. This was definitely reserved for the Western Hemisphere. And the old-world horses did not bring it with them. Its origin is unquestionably due to some sound physical cause generated in America. Cougar attacks are the most probable.

"Bucking," by the way, is a word that originated in the North. It is thought to have derived from "buckaroo," which is, in turn, the Northwest's version of "vaquero." As the average working buckaroo's horses were usually inclined to shake out a few kinks on frosty mornings, it was only logical that his mounts should reflect an allusion to his name. Thus we have "buckers" and "bucking."

The word drifted across the continental divide, where it spread down into the central plains to meet its counterpart, "pitching," which came up from the South. "Pitching" originated in the Southwest. It was used almost exclusively from Arizona to Texas. "Bucking" was seldom heard in that country until after 1890, while "pitching" never did gain much of a hold north of Cheyenne. The two words met and mingled on the central plains in the trail-driving days of the late 1880s, where they were later used more or less indiscriminately.

The Spanish horse, which created the devilish art that meant the same in any language, differed little throughout the West. Nor was he by any means unknown in the East. Countless herds were rounded up and driven into the farming regions east of the Missouri and Mississippi. There, they were delivered to eastern horse markets or auctioned off from town to town. Some even reached the Atlantic states while a few were taken abroad. Usually rough broken during their eastward journey, they filled a need for saddle ponies and driving stock among those who didn't harbor the idea that anything wearing a brand was an unconquerable demon possessed by all the savagery of the wilderness.

An old sea-captain friend from the Maine coast once told me of one such animal that was owned near his hometown during early times. The mustang never exhibited any particular meanness in his task of pulling a farmer's cart. But he wore a big Cross Bar T on his hip, which had all the damning significance of a bottle-shaped bulge in the pocket of the town's disgrace. Never did the local residents get over viewing him as something akin to a scalp-hungry Sioux or a Texas badman. "A branded critter in that country," my friend insisted, "excited people's imaginations worse than a Nick Carter novel."

It was much the same in varying degrees through all the eastern farming sections during the late 1800s and early 1900s. The mustang was usually viewed with suspicion by those whose minds were trained to narrow horizons and provincial viewpoints. This, combined with the soil-tilling footman's habitually inferiority-haunted distrust of a freewheeling horseman's world, fostered an aversion, if not fear, toward both men and beast from the wild, unfettered lands beyond the Missouri.

But the mustangs which traveled afar soon lost their identity under the influence of kinder environments and infusions of gentler blood. This tended to create a more tractable nature with an increase in size and corresponding decrease in vitality. Those who knew them in their foreign setting never realized the true nature of the indestructible little beasts which roamed the plains.

Andy Adams wrote that he had seen adult mustangs of his acquaintance gain as much as two hundred pounds in weight and several inches in height after a couple of years on the northern ranges. With this, a desire for heavier horses in the mountainous regions and dual-purpose settler stock worked toward satisfying man's innate desire to remodel anything nature created for a special purpose. All this led to a need for better treatment, richer feed, and more-lenient demands for hardiness. By the time the horsemeat dealers and gasoline producers got into the act, the mustang was on his way out.

Various breeders have expended considerable effort in trying to develop strains that will give modern horses some of the mustang's lost qualities. Some of them have had fair success with quarter-horse and Arabian crosses. Quite a few of these have demonstrated in late years a rebirth of the old speed, endurance, and cow-sense of the pioneer breed. Further improvements look most promising. But it is a question whether the modern world can ever produce the special qualities that nature and environment infused into that tough little creature which circulated the lifeblood of America's Old West.

Among the old-timers, especially in the Southwest, the old Spanish names for horse colors are still everyday expressions in rangeland lingo. Mention of a *bayo* would mean a dun; should he also have a black mane and tail, he would be a *bayo cabo negro*. An orange-colored dun is a *bayo maranjado*. *Colorado* designates the reddish bay, while a golden bay would be a *dorado*. *Alazan* stands for a plain sorrel; *rosillo* for a red one. Grays and grizzly colors would be *tordillos*. *Prieto* and *blanco* mean black and white respectively. Paints or spotted animals are the well-known *pintos*. *Palomino* means dove-colored.

The name "palomino" is also believed by some researchers to have derived from the name of a certain Juan Palamia, who accompanied the de Anza expedition to California in 1774. Palamia is recorded as having ridden a golden stallion on the journey. The supposition is that this animal sowed a few wild oats among the mares brought north by the colonists. The family bloodline thus deposited resulted in an occasional golden colt appearing among the mustang herds of later years. If such was the actual case, there would be little ground left under the feet of those who contend that the palomino is merely a freak color phase rather than a basic breed.

On the other hand, it would do much to strengthen the theory held by many students of the subject that the palomino heritage runs back into antiquity. The latter faction believes these were the golden horses with fair manes and tails mentioned in the Homeric poems as the animals that carried the Greek demigods to victory. Various historical references link them with a breed famous among the Chaldeans and an equally noted strain bred for beauty, speed, and color by the Saracens. There is little reason to doubt that there was a special breed of horses, at least very similar to the palominos, renowned among the ancient nobility of the East. In the early centuries of the Christian era we hear of the golden horse appearing farther west, quite likely transported from Saracen lands.

According to some authorities, the Golden Ones were fairly plentiful among the Arabs until about 600 A.D. While the Arabs admired them greatly as horses, they found their striking color to be a serious disadvantage in battle. A warrior so mounted had about as much chance to avoid hostile attention as a British lobsterback trying to slip through the ranks of Ethan Allen's Minutemen. What with trying to conquer their western neighbors and being at war most of the time, the Arabs made a systematic effort to get rid of the horses so attractive to enemy eyes. They eventually bred them out of existence among their herds.

But it was either a potent strain or a new seed sprouted up from other quarters. Barb mares taken to Spain by the Moorish conquerors brought the breed into focus again by dropping an occasional golden colt. The gold-loving Spaniards regarded such animals as gifts from heaven, rating them as badges of royalty. Following the departure of the Moors, they called them "Ysabellas" in honor of the queen who succeeded in freeing the country. But they were extremely rare. By the time of the Spanish conquest in America, there were still only a few of the golden animals in Spain. However, Isabella sent a stud and five mares to the viceroy in Mexico as a start toward propagating the breed in the New World.

History is not very explicit about how this experiment worked out. Apparently, the Spaniards in Mexico let nature take its course rather than make much effort at selective breeding. Palominos seem to have run mainly to isolated individuals all through the two hundred years of Mexican expansion.

It was the same in early California. Colts appeared from time to time among the free-ranging herds. They were eagerly sought and, when caught, highly prized. Seldom would a caballero part with such a treasure once it fell into his possession. In fact, it even became sort of an unwritten rule among the Californios that such animals could not be sold. As a gift, yes, on a par with giving a daughter in marriage or a herd of cattle to an impoverished relative; but no one would ever dream of selling one.

Yet, little attention seems to have been given to building up the strain. Then, when the Americans moved in, the majority of whom were farmers and tradesmen blessed with a fine disdain for anything pertaining to Mexicans in general and the easy going caballeros in particular, they viewed the native horses as something to get rid of, or crossbreed with eastern stock to make them look more like something from back home. So it was that after a thousand years of delight to the horseman's eye, the late 1800s found this handsome breed once more almost faded into oblivion.

But they lived on. Rembrandt immortalized them in oil as the Chinese did in water colors; modern artists and writers often pictured them against the background of the New World; old-timers drew on their memories for fleeting visions of golden skins and flowing silver manes. The occasional palomino that did appear usually passed into the hands of some speculative owner with the soul of an artist and memories of past glories.

Thus there was a thin scattering of seed stock dotting the Southwest when a few particularly understanding horsemen began reviving dreams of restoring the golden breed in the early 1900s. In the late 1920s, these few were joined by others who, by dint of careful inbreeding and crossing with certain types of Arabians, plus a fabulous amount of money, finally succeeded in establishing antiquity's Mounts of the Gods as a definite class among America's choice saddle-horse breeds.

It was the less pretentious, but no less sturdy, descendants of Cordoban horses that carried most of the trailblazing soldiers and settlers up into California from Mexico following the original penetration in 1769. Once established, these animals spread over the country west of the Sierra Nevadas in the same manner displayed on the southern plains. Some idea of their affinity for the warm valleys of the West may be gained from the fact that the two hundred horses and mules belonging to the five pioneer California missions in 1773 had increased to 61,600 distributed among the twenty-one missions of 1834.

Meanwhile, the same expansion had been going on among the new ranchos springing up from San Diego to San Francisco. Thousands of the mustangs roamed the sprawling land grants and outlying territories. A large part ranged at will, untended and uncounted. The old Californios were a freehanded lot. There were horses enough for all, and to spare. Why worry about numbers or range limits? Some neighbor's horses were usually available if his own were out of reach; and who was to mind if a friend appropriated a few of his for temporary use?

Moreover, when some young man without adequate funds desired to start a spread, it was regarded as only common courtesy to let him round up a bunch of mares from whatever outside stock he could find and have them as a loan until he got a herd started for himself. The mares would be returned, or replaced in like numbers with young stock, as soon as the new ranchero had raised a satisfactory supply of his own animals. The benefactor reasoned that such a procedure was merely a helpful gesture from one who had more than he needed. Besides, with the loan sure to be returned, he wouldn't be losing anything. What could be fairer? And it all made for agreeable associations in a land where pleasant living was an accomplished art.

There was only one bad feature connected with such a system, or lack of system: When the Americans began penetrating the Sierras from the East in the early 1800s, they discovered an exceptional strain of horses in the western valleys. Whether these animals had developed from a better class of stock than those that came north into Arizona and New Mexico, or resulted from feed and climatic conditions, is a matter of opinion—and considerable spirited discussion. The fact remains, however, that the western horses immediately captured the attention of all visitors from the East. The Californios were also rich in as fine a grade of mules as could be found anywhere.

By 1830, such horsetraders as Ewing Young, David Jackson, and William Wolfskill were making frequent pilgrimages from New Mexico to buy herds of the superior California animals for trade in Santa Fe and among the rapidly increasing trailblazers.

Various unscrupulous individuals were soon eyeing this highly lucrative trade with greedy attention. Lacking money to buy stock, their devious minds turned to less-laudable methods. Armed with the common knowledge of the Californios' loosely managed ranching practices, they simply rode over the mountains and helped themselves to any unguarded herds they might find. Thousands of fine horses and mules were thus rounded up and driven out of the territory without the owners being aware of it until too late. Thousands more were stolen openly under cover of murderous gunfire. Such raids did much to promote the hostility many Californios later harbored toward Americans.

It was from these California mustangs that the coastal valleys of the Pacific Northwest obtained a large share of their original saddle stock and stage horses. The settlers of the old Oregon Territory arrived in the most part by ox teams. The few horses they brought with them ran mostly to draft animals and a scattering of saddle mounts from the East's farming regions. By and large, these immigrants were agriculturists, caring little for the wide, free horizons of true horsemen. As a mater of fact, riding horses seldom assumed any outstanding importance in their perspective. Nevertheless, travel in the new land was mostly by way of narrow Indian trails or over unmarked territory. On horseback or on foot was the only practicable way to get about. Those who didn't care for the heavy gait of the family farm horse soon began looking for something more suitable to the saddle. The sturdy, easy-gaited mustang from the South seemed to be the answer.

At least, they appealed to the newly arrived settlers more than did the half-wild Indian ponies of the upper Columbia and Snake River plains, which was the only other convenient source of supply. The California animals were usually fairly well trained to the saddle before reaching Oregon. They also seemed to have some kind of a mental heritage that made them more adaptable to the settlers' ideas of equine decorum.

There were some of the Spanish horses around the Fort Vancouver region of the lower Columbia River when the new settlers began arriving. American mountain-men and Hudson's Bay Company trappers had started working down into California around 1825. Many of them developed a preference for the southern animals, which they acquired by trade or less-laudable means and brought back north with them. All experienced horsemen recognized the worth of such horses in a pioneer wilderness and were anxious to mount themselves in a like manner.

It was still only 1836 when popular demand induced the new-born Willamette Cattle Company to send the far-ranging Western Trader, Ewing Young, to California for the purpose of buying horses and cattle for the budding settlement at Oregon City. The forty mustangs which Young purchased at San Jose Mission, along with 727 head of cattle, were trailed back to the Willamette Valley to form the first permanent cornerstone in West Coast saddle-horse development. The success of this move sparked further importations to meet the needs of expanding settlement. The most notable of the following ventures was, perhaps, that of Joseph Gale and Felix Hathaway. They trailed 600 horses and mules, 1,250 cattle, and 3,000 sheep to the lower Willamette Valley in 1843.

Time and increasing population served to spread this western mustang through all the coastal valleys as far north as British Columbia. During the following decades, he filled the limited needs for saddle and driving horses usually present in an agricultural country. It remained for the gentler, more stylish encroachments of eastern importations to shove him out of the picture.

Of no less importance was the mustang migration which moved northward east of the Sierra-Cascade Mountains. As noted in the chapter on Indian horses, this infusion was quite comparable to that of the Great Plains, reaching the North even earlier. Herds, both wild and semidomesticated by the Indians, were there to greet the first white venturers into little-known Nevada, Utah, western Colorado, and the inland empire of the Pacific Northwest. The high plateau sections of eastern Washington and Oregon and southern Idaho were especially rich in mustangs when we opened the first pages of western history.

Although the Utes and Snakes were the first northern people to acquire them, the greatest concentration of horses and probably the greatest horsemen around the close of the eighteenth century were found in the country of the Cayuse, Walla Walla, and Nez Percé. They all received their original mustangs from the Snakes somewhere around 1730. A statement to that effect was made by an aged Nez Percé whom Captain Meriwether Lewis met on the Clearwater River of Idaho in 1805. Other evidence coincides very well with the old Indian's memory. The animals were thriving in great abundance on the rich grasslands of that section when Lewis first arrived there.

SIOUX PAD SADDLE

While traveling up the Columbia River to establish Fort Spokane, Alexander Ross wrote in his journal for August 12, 1812, of encountering a camp of Indians at the mouth of the Walla Walla River. He said the surrounding prairie was literally covered with horses. According to his estimate, ". . . There could not have been less than 4,000 within sight of the camp." That this was nothing unusual is evinced by similar observations made by several early visitors to that section.

It was these mustangs which furnished the saddle stock for the great cattle empire that sprang up between the Rockies and the Cascades in the middle 1800s. And it was they, like their cousins on the Great Plains, who served the needs of an empire in the making and went on to bequeath their heritage to the succeeding generations of cow horses, saddlers, and road animals so necessary to a country of great distances and individual enterprise.

This branch of the mustang family, like the original mustangs everywhere, had all the outstanding characteristics which make the breed a legend that will live forever throughout the West. It is difficult for those of today, who never had the advantage of knowing the unique animal, to appreciate its remarkable endurance, intelligence, surefootedness, courage, rawhide strength, and ability to do any required job on a minimum of food. Even in its heyday, people who had not actually associated with the breed were more than a little skeptical of its storied abilities.

A typical case was the Easterner, an experienced horseman, who came to the West with a mind frankly antagonistic to any suggestions of mustang superiority. Before his trip was over, he wrote his enforced change of opinion as: ". . . in favor of the native stock. They are of good size, not too heavy, strong and full of spirit, remarkably free travelers, and possessing the most wonderful powers of endurance I have ever seen."

As with most Easterners, however, only firsthand experience could make a believer out of him.

The most outstanding member of the mustang family was the Nez Percé horse. It was already a highly developed and well-established breed when white men first entered its territory surrounding the present Lewiston, Idaho. One of the great mysteries of the Northwest is this animal's origin and the native horsemanship which developed and maintained it from a time that no one knows. Although the full story is lost in Indian antiquity, there is little doubt that the strain started with some Spanish horse possessing unique and most remarkable qualities. Some students of the subject believe it was a throwback to a special breed of ancient

Persia, rising through bloodstreams that flowed westward through Africa, Spain, and Mexico to the Pacific Northwest. From there on it was simply a matter of intelligent breeding principles and good management.

When Lewis and Clark traversed the Nez Percé country in 1805, the former wrote that this nation was more expert in breeding fine horses than any Virginia horsemen of his acquaint-

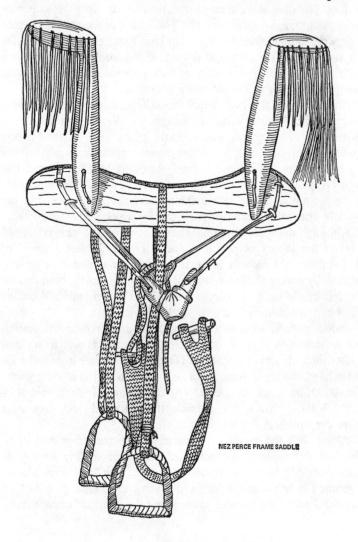

NEZ PERCE FRAME SADDLE

ance. Also, that their horses were superior to any horses he had previously known.

Succeeding travelers through that country all told the same story, as well as voicing the like opinion of Indian acquaintances throughout the West. The Nez Percé horse, with its peculiarly spotted rump, appealed to everyone as the mount par excellence for anyone who wanted intelligence, speed, stamina, and sureness of foot. Standing at an average of fifteen hands high, these animals were fairly large-bodied and had good lung capacity. Their front legs were rather close together, making them especially valuable on narrow trails and rough terrain. Good conformity combined with their knowledgeable ways and exceptional agility made them unequaled as war or buffalo-running horses.

The heart of the Nez Percé horse's homeland was the lush valley of the Palouse River in southeastern Washington. It is from there that he takes his name. Early white men in that region quite naturally set the distinctive animal apart from his fellows by calling him "a Palouse horse." Assorted tongues slurred this into "Appalousie," "Palousie," or simply "Loosy." American linguistics were not long in bunching these several names into the equally distinctive word "Appaloosa," by which he is still known.

Although there are doubting Thomases who look with jaundiced eyes at the theory of primitives actually establishing a breed of this stature, old records leave little question that it was accomplished by a very skillful system of selective breeding, bounded on the left by the judicious disposal of inferior individuals and on the right by the old law of survival of the fittest.

Indian nature, as a whole, precluded any great consideration for weakness in man or beast. Horses were a means to an end rather than objects of attention. They treated them rough and rode them hard, having a thought for only those which made the grade. As Ross Cox wrote in speaking of the Palouse Indians in 1811–12: "Without doubt, the animals that survived such treatment were the strongest and toughest of all."

Along with the sacrifice to nature of the weaklings and unfit, the Nez Percé made a practice of selling or trading only their least-desirable horses from year to year. The best ones always remained in tribal hands for perpetuating their kind. Fortified by the rich feed of the Palouse country and the demand for endurance that outranges the experience of any modern horseman, it was only natural that the Appaloosa advanced to where it was prized above any other mount by all men, white or red, west of the Missouri River.

Long before the coming of Europeans, and for many years afterward, Nez Percé horses were unexcelled as the choicest items for barter around all the big Indian trade centers. At The Dalles of the Columbia they brought the highest returns in exchange for dried or smoked salmon, dried berries, seashells, shell ornaments, and other coast products. East of the Rockies they were never without takers in trade for Sioux warbonnets and weapons, Crow buffalo robes and beaded garments, Arapaho horn spoons and implements, Minnesota pipestone, Missouri Valley corn and dried fruits, and riding gear from California. Altogether, it is not too much to envision the horses with oddly spotted rumps as occasional lustrous gems, like choice beads interspersed on a string, dotting the far-flung threads of Indian trade routes that twined from the Pacific to the Atlantic and from Mexico to Canada. Even to this day, there are few Indians alive who are not pushovers for the unparalleled war horse, the wonder steed with unbelievable endurance.

Taking the country as a whole, there must have been a considerable number of them scattered over the West. Early observers in all parts of the country mentioned them frequently. Warriors of all nations coveted them as war or hunting mounts. Many white men preferred them to any other horses. Old Bill Williams's Appaloosa horse was almost as famous as he himself. Contemporary artists usually included representations of the breed in their western paintings. Charles M. Russell's Indian pictures of a somewhat later date seldom lack a Nez Percé horse among the mounted subjects.

The Nez Percé themselves were ever rich in the better examples of the breed whose bloodlines they had guarded through the ages. The Lewis and Clark journals speak with frank wonder at the quantity and quality of horses encountered there. Father de Smet, after visiting these people in 1845, said he often found as many as fifteen hundred head in the possession of individual families. Franchere, Cox, Ross, and many others voiced similar statements in their accounts of Nez Percé horse culture. Most of them mentioned the owners' reluctance to part with the choicer animals.

It remained for the brains of the U. S. War Department to sweep this ancient and extraordinary breed almost into oblivion overnight. This was the final act in the so-called Nez Percé War of 1877.

As a matter of fact, it was a war only in the minds of the army's glory hunters and a few settlers; but Young Chief Joseph didn't know that. He just wanted to move his people up into Canada, where he understood treaty-making was a more reliable institution. Naturally, he took all the tribe's choice horses along, the same as any emigrant would take the family treasures with him upon moving to a new land. But the army didn't have what it took to understand that. All it could think of was revenge for having to stay out in the cold weather and chase 431 Indians—over half of which were women and children—for thirteen hundred miles through three states while absorbing five sound shellackings in the process. When they finally cornered the little half-starved band in the Bear Paw Mountains of Montana, where they had camped and gone to sleep, thinking they were safely over the line into Canada, they promptly shot most of the irreplaceable horses in self-adjudged retaliation for their masters' crime of trying to save their own scalps without bloodshed.

During this same period, the killing of Indian horses as an aid to forcing the natives up to the ration counter was in effect all over the country. General Wright had instituted the order to shoot all such animals on sight, after having his dignity wounded by Indians who outrode, outmaneuvered, and outfought his troops all along the line. The spotted Appaloosa being the favorite war horse of the more influential and aggressive Indian leaders throughout the West, it naturally received the most direct attention. By the time the natives were made to see the great shining light of governmental benevolence, the Nez Percé horse was almost as bad off as its masters. What few remained received scant notice from the white settlers, who were prone to regard anything pertaining to Indians as something to be despised.

Had it not been for a thin scattering of very sensible and particularly enlightened horsemen, this famous breed might well have followed the heath hen and passenger pigeon into extinction.

Thanks to those few, a nucleus of the animals was preserved to stage a slow and belated comeback after about 1935. Now again receiving the wholehearted respect of knowledgeable horse lovers, we may hope that succeeding generations of scientific breeders will bring them in some measure back to the prominence they enjoyed under the tutelage of unlettered red men.

*Chapter XIII*

## THE WAY OF THE COWBOY

In looking at the cowboy we see a breed as distinctive as the mustang horse and the longhorn steer. And like the mustang and the longhorn, he is, as a whole, forever inimitable and unalterable. You may adulterate certain of his characteristics, plaster him with a veneer of environment, or disguise him in foreign garb, but the man himself remains as he always was—a cowboy. It shows in his walk, in his actions, and in the way he wears his clothes. You can see it in his eyes, in the set of his feet, and the tilt of his hat. And although he may have wandered far, the echo of pounding hoofs and lonesome trails will ever lurk in the background of his voice for all discerning ears to hear. As E. C. (Teddy Blue) Abbott so aptly put it, "I would know an old cowbody in hell with his hide burnt off."

The cowboy cannot be imitated with any success. Others may wear his clothes and mouth his words, but only as glaring impostors in the eyes of the initiate. And it is rightly so. No man is more true to his heritage, a heritage which sprang from the ancient Sarmatians to flow through Tartars, Parthians, Persians, Hungarians, Moors, and Spaniards. His traditions are as old as human history and carry all the emphasis of equites, knights, equerries, chevaliers, cavaliers, and caballeros. The silvery tinkle of his spurs and the proud tapping of his feet repeat a cadence that has echoed down through the halls of time since the dawn of civilization. His voice, his hands, his legs, his gestures, the buoyant swagger in his walk, the unconscious gallantry in his behavior, his bold vices, and his unpretentious virtues reflect the unmistakable bearing of a man chosen by fate to move on a somewhat higher plane than that of his earthbound neighbors.

His pride is perhaps his greatest single characteristic, no doubt born of his ability to control the silken-skinned power, which, pressed between his knees, carries him to heights undreamed of by any footman. He is proud of his appearance, his independence, his skill, his ability to meet all contingencies, his outfit, and his way of life. Though a laborer he may be, working for hire, he never considers himself a hired man, or even a laborer in the common sense of the word. Instead, he is a helping hand there to assist the man who pays his wages. He takes pride in his ability to do whatever becomes necessary in his line of duties and to conduct his efforts without supervision by a boss. His craft, like that of no other profession, allows him to express his independence in thought and action, to go and come as he pleases, to be, in short, a gentleman on horseback—a true cavalier in all that the name implies. Sensitive, soft-spoken, vain, polite, trustworthy, egotistical, clannish, self-sufficient, observant, practical, imaginative, with the soul of an artist and the spirit of a nobleman, he stands as the end product of eight millennia of horse-borne royalty.

Although he would probably be the last person in the world to admit it, he is at heart an unrivaled beauty lover. This is expressed in the richly worked inlays of his bridle bits and spurs, the elaborate designs carved on his saddle, the silver or nickel conchos and spots that trim his chaps, belts, and cuffs, the brightly colored shirts, silk mufflers, and finely turned boots reserved for holiday attire. Nature is his home, bounded by flower-dotted stretches of emerald prairies and the fantastic panorama of sharply etched mountains outlined against the painted murals of flaming sunsets. To see him forget everything while feasting his eyes on the clean symmetry of a horse, or halt involuntarily on the crest of a hill as the splendor of some unspoiled landscape suddenly unrolls before him, is to sense the spirit of the true aesthetic. Ordinarily denied the opportunity to create artificial beauty, he rides hand in hand with the Creator himself, overlooking little that was designed to enrich the soul of man. Largely inarticulate in the face of sentiment, he would more than likely only admit, "It's shore plumb handsome," and let it go at that. You have only to catch that look of a well-satisfied connoisseur, however, to know that true appreciation can easily dispense with words.

By the same token, his affinity with nature reflects itself in a close kinship with the Great Designer. Often unconsciously and ever laconically, he is prone to regard the sun, moon, and stars, the rivers, mountains, and plains, the regular flow of the seasons, and the yearly mystery of life as being merely unexplainable parts of a Divine pattern scattered along his trail as guideposts to an unquestioned hereafter.

An old hardshell cowboy friend of mine once summed it up very neatly in one of his rare moments of loquacity: "Nobody'd ever make the mistake o' cuttin' me in with the religious bunch," he said. "Fellers like us just don't grade out for that market. But livin' as we do, with the animals and the growin' things, and everything having a right to live, we know you've got to play your hand with all the cards on the table if yo' aim to stand up as half a man. And when thoughts of all the wonders wrapped up in these here mountains, prairies, and that great blue yonder up above move in to whittle yo' down to the little wart o' nothing yo' really are, it makes you dang glad the Big Boss who staked out the whole deal is out there ridin' herd till time for the Big Roundup."

And while waiting for the Big Roundup, the cowboy, like all horsemen of all ages, treasures his freedom, the land in which he lives, and the way of life he has chosen for his own above all material wealth. Nobody ever heard of a cowboy wanting to join a union or elect a smooth-talking outsider to manage his personal affairs. It is his greatest desire to be far removed from fume-loaded air, rabbit-hutch congestion, welfare regimentation, robot routines, nagging solicitors, parking meters, mug shots, serial numbers, licenses, permits, registrations, and all officious petty-office holders who would pry into where he is from, what he is doing, and where he expects to go, while tapping his habitually lean purse for the flowery promise of a doubtful future dreamed up by some assembly-line god who would have everybody shaped to his own image.

The country where he works may be a raw and inhospitable land, but the cowboy would not exchange it for any soft, pampered region on earth. Although his life is hard, exacting, and beset by a host of dangers, long hours, and the contrarieties of nature, he is perfectly happy with it. Men of all other professions are continually on the move, looking for that elusive Utopia of dreams. Other institutions usually are in a perpetual state of unrest over everything from better labor relations to better access to the government pork barrel. But none of these things breeds ulcers for the cowboy and cattleman. They already have what they want—the good life. They have no urge to migrate. Neither do they care to make their country over into a gargantuan grab-bag which would eventually smother them in its folds. No, the cowman is happy here and now. All he asks is that the costly and unworkable encumbrances under which the rest of the country labors not be thrust upon him by dictatorial do-gooders.

It is true that the man who follows cattle is often dogged by heartbreaking difficulties. Often poor in worldly goods, the operations of nature and financial manipulators may grind him down to a whisper. Yet all he asks is more of the same without outside interference. His is a big country, and he is a big man; he figures he will make out. The main thing is to stand on his own feet with the courage that will insure his beloved freedom. If he has a few extra dollars, he buys a new saddle or a pair of boots and goes to a dance. Lacking the extra dollars, he goes to the dance anyway, and enjoys every minute of it. Nobody ever saw a despondent cowboy, or one subjected to the sweet agony of a psychiatrist's couch.

Such a contented outlook on life gives the cowboy the impression that he is different from more circumscribed men found around him. This leads to a sense of well-being which, upon looking down from the back of his mount, flares up in the traditional horseman's feeling of superiority. Others tend to take him at his own valuation and accept the world he has built around himself as an established concern. Thus, his characteristics have been carried around the globe to present him as the one real American, who, even more than the figure of Uncle Sam, exemplifies the romance of the Western world and remains unchanged throughout the convulsions of progressive civilization.

No other occupation has had so many words written about it, nor been pictured so extensively in so many ways. The entire world has never taken any other single figure to its heart as it has the American cowboy. Half the magazines, movies, and TV productions would wither on the vine if denied use of his exploits. An astonishing percentage of sports-clothing manufacturers, toy factories, and vacation promoters would have to go out of business if a ban were put on cowboy gear, dude ranches, and rodeo performances. Even commercial advertising would lose a large share of its appeal without a cowboy in the foreground to sing the praises of certain products.

No outsider quite understands it. It is always hard for the world to comprehend a man who is fully contented with his lot. Equally hard to grasp is the idea that the West is not something which can be learned; it must be absorbed by degrees over a period of time.

Perhaps that is why so many eastern urbanites, when they deal with western subjects, find themselves relegated to the bottom shelf by native Westerners. The true brand of the West is an element that grows from the inside out. It cannot be dubbed on nor appropriated by the casual visitor. And although certain ones, unseasoned by the cowcountry, may have all the right words in the right places, the result will all too often resemble an old, mossyhorn cowboy who thinks a suit of store-bought clothes will set him up as a sophisticated man-about-town.

Much of this misinterpretation comes from the all-too-common attitude toward the way the cowboy outfits himself. The idea that the big hat, loosely tied bandanna, heavy chaps, spurs, and high-heeled boots are mere affectations assumed for show is a simple case of unenlightened provincialism. The belittling allusions occasionally made by those who should know better are shining examples of ignorance on parade.

It is understood, of course, that we are talking about the cowboy; not the stuffed shirt in cowboy clothes.

Everything this working man on horseback wears, uses, or does has a logical purpose developed over more than a century of practical experience. The fact that he usually wears a similar style of clothing as social or business dress is only another manifestation of his determination to be himself in the face of a civilization which swings with the pendulum of fashion to all points of the compass. From his viewpoint, the eccentric is never the fellow who sticks to what is best for him, but the one who can't build a culture of his own.

Why should he succumb to the implication that his hat is a monstrosity designed for dramatic exhibition, when he knows it is the most suitable headgear yet designed for his profession? It serves all the purpose of an umbrella in rain, snow, and blazing sunshine. Many a cowboy has escaped serious injury when afoot by having that big hat to slap in the face of a mad cow-brute bent on destruction. Thrown in front of a runaway horse or a spooky bunch-quitter trying to dodge a corral gate, it often saves a hard chase after the miscreant. Held in the free hand while riding a bucker, it serves much the same purpose as a balance pole in the hands of a high-wire walker, or it can be swung against the animal's head to guide it away from dangerous objects. It is a handy substitute for a water bucket, to dip water out of a creek or water a horse. It will shield the cowboy's face from frost or dew while he sleeps or the heat and smoke from a cranky campfire while he eats breakfast. It will take the place of a basket when he picks a bouquet for his best girl or discovers a hen's stolen nest down in the back pasture. It will cover most of his perishable possessions when the bunkhouse roof threatens to leak before morning or keep them off the damp ground when sleeping outside. And under all conditions, it gives him a prideful sense of well-being to have such a substantial, attractively built crown for his wardrobe, a heritage from the plumed hats and embellished helmets allotted only to history's men on horseback.

The cotton bandanna, or large silk muffler, is even more versatile. Tied loosely around the neck, it is always available for whatever emergency arises, yet is never an added encumbrance. Primarily, it was intended to shield his neck from the sun, but it could be pulled up over the nose and cheeks, like a mask, to protect the face from winter blizzards or burning desert winds. In the dust-choked arena of a branding corral or behind the churning feet of a trail herd it served as a respirator. The cowboy might use it for a towel after washing his face in some waterhole, or for tying his hat down over his ears when facing a storm. It made a blindfold for a spooky bronc, a pigging string for tying down an odd calf to be branded, a sling for a broken arm, a bandage for a wound, or a towel for drying a few camp dishes.

Spread over dirty water, it could be used as a strainer to drink through; wrung out of cold water and stuffed into his hat, it would keep his head cool; dry, it might be tied around the ears under his hat on frosty mornings. It was often used in bundling up small objects for safekeeping, to piece out a short rope for tying up a bedroll, replace a broken belt, substitute for a bridle head-stall, tie the legs of a stray dogie while packing it to the ranch, or to wrap around the handle of a hot frying pan while cooking supper. It was a handy thing to use for signaling; men have been hung with it; and it has covered the face of many a dead cowboy whose career ended on the bare, unsettled prairies. J. Frank Dobie voices the opinion of many old-timers when he says, "The bandanna deserves to be called the flag of the cowcountry."

Curtailed ranges, shorter riding journeys, and better supplies of needed articles combined to lessen the ever-present demands for bandannas. Although still commonly worn for everyday use, the 1914–16 period found many of the boys substituting a long, narrow type for dress-up wear. They were tied around the neck above the shirt collar with a foot or so of ends left to hang down. Later years have seen even this remnant of the old bandanna discarded in many places. But out on the range among working cowboys it is still not an uncommon adjunct—and it is not worn to impress any chance visitor gathering atmosphere from the window of a passing bus.

If that same visitor labors under any delusion that the cowboy he sees loping out through the sagebrush is wearing chaps merely to make himself look like a vest-pocket edition of Buffalo Bill, he is grossly mistaken. Chaps are a very essential item of equip-ment for men on the range, despite the fact that Western-movie actors have pretty well discarded them in order to show off their finely tailored saddle pants. Cowboys like their pants, too. That's why they wear chaps. Nothing better than chaps has ever been devised for protecting a rider from cactus, barbwire, brush, rope burns, horses' teeth, and sideswiping cow horns. This time-proven garment also sheds rain, snow, and the ever-present range dust; it furnishes warmth in cold weather, driving storms, and bitter wind. Its leather-to-leather surface against the saddle holds better than cloth pants when riding a bucker, while any cowboy is aware that the skin he saves may be his own if he is wearing chaps when a horse falls on him or perhaps spreads him out over a rocky hillside.

If he is wearing spurs, there is a fair chance that he may avoid the latter accident. Spurs are not ornaments; they are working tools. With them clamped against the heavy cinch, he probably would have been able to ride it out; spurs are a wonderful aid in helping to keep a man's posterior from soaring above the saddle. But more important, with these jingling reminders swaying gently beside its ribs, the horse likely would never have tried impromptu shenanigans in the first place. Horses are taught to respect spurs. A good rider transmits many of his orders to a mount by light touches of the rowels. This is especially true when his hands are busy with a rope or other employment. The horse soon learns to respond to their gentle urging, to turn or go as their promptings indicate. Obstinate and willful animals likewise soon come to understand that the wages of delinquency are on a pair of raking heels ready to change current principles of conduct. None of this is done cruelly or for brutal torture by knowledgeable cowboys. Any worthwhile rangeman thinks a lot of his horses and acts accordingly. He uses spurs as he does the bit or whip, more as a handy reminder than as actual punishment. And the fact that he often has them made in elaborate and fanciful designs is due to his innate love of beauty, not to any desire to entertain refugees from the subway district.

His spurs are fitting accompaniments to those finely worked boots, whose slim toes and high, tapering heels are so often the butt of cheap jokes fostered by a certain class of minds. Such boots are the result of decades of trial and experimentation by men who accept only the best for their specialized craft. The slender toe is shaped to pick up a swinging stirrup with ease, or to release it with equal ease if necessary. The high heel prevents the foot from going through the stirrup while allowing comfort of riding with the weight supported by the specially constructed arch. The heel is also slanted forward to serve as an anchor when its wearer braces against a critter on the end of his rope when afoot. The high, stiff counter is designed to carry the spur without discomfort, while the smooth instep has no eyelets, hooks, laces, knots, or buckles to bruise the foot or mar its smooth fit against the stirrup. The high tops guard against snakes, thorns, barbwire, lashing storms, and the ugly teeth of an occasional bronc who feels the urge for a taste of human flesh. Overall, it is a fine-looking piece of footwear, adding dignity to the wearer who takes pride in his appearance. That is why it, like the cowboy's hat, is so often chosen by the ordinary western citizen and his visiting eastern cousin for everyday wear.

Like the Indian, the cowboy inhabits a world of his own. He has his own language, customs, humor, principles, ways of doing things, and manner of thinking. He attaches a name of his own choosing to a stranger and evaluates that person by his own standards. Anyone who enters his domain must accommodate himself to existing conditions and take what is set before him. It is he, not the cowboy, who is looking for something he doesn't have.

All this is not an attempt, however, to paint the cowboy as a paragon of virtue or a phenomenon of good judgment. Basically, he is a wild, tough individual of uncertain and often violet temperament. He is often described as being so full of contrary independence that if he fell into a river, he would swim upstream to get out. This fierce independence usually induces him to fight his own battles and, on occasion, to take the law into his own hands. Living close to the violence of nature, as he does, this frequently results in outbursts that border on primeval savagery. Too, long weeks of living alone, with only dumb brutes and the elements for company, tend to bottle up emotions that explode in unpredictable ways when opportunity presents an occasional holiday.

This particular phase of his character is the one that has caused the greatest general misunderstanding of the cowboy. Most of the townspeople of the West, from earliest pioneer times, were men on foot; usually transplanted Easterners, to boot. As such, they knew little and cared less about the cowboy's background of thought and action. Perhaps this was the natural reaction of earth-bound men forced to look upward toward a swifter and more-dashing being enjoying the enviable freedom denied those of prosaic conventionality. Or perhaps it was the plain inability of small men to see beyond their own shadows. At any rate, their knowledge of the cowboy was largely confined to what they saw of his unrestrained moments in town. These were the brief interludes when accumulated days of heat, drought, loneliness, and long hours in the saddle could be forgotten in the exuberance of youthful spirits released. They saw him gambling away his hard-earned wages and saturating himself with liquor at the town-sponsored saloons, but they overlooked the months of drabness and unswerving toil that fermented the outburst. They observed his often-unprintable language, earthy humor, and coarse horse-play without inquiring into the fact that he would straitjacket every fun-loving instinct he possessed rather than embarrass a respectable woman or abuse a child. Many uncharitable words were heaped upon his head because of his propensity for periodical visits to the gilded houses of joy, the only place where he might ordinarily assuage his longing for a bit of feminine companionship, yet few took note of the fact that any virtuous woman was as safe in his company as if guarded by a company of church deacons and two old-maid aunts. Seldom did anyone bother to analyze the courage and staunchness which often caused him to battle fire, flood, or blizzard twenty-four hours a day to protect his employer's herds, or even face death at gunpoint in the interest of his boss—all for forty dollars a month. His long hours on night herd, the riding down stampedes in rain-lashed darkness, the dust-fogged miles all the way up from Texas held no interest for conventional urban minds, but their clamor could be heard for a mile against a hard wind if he let off a little steam by whooping it up and shooting a few holes in the atmosphere when he came to town.

This particular type of pastime happened to be based on an old and very sensible custom in use long before the makers of western towns came out of their sheltered East. Among the native Indians, it was a sign of peace for any peaceful visitors to announce themselves by giving out with a chorus of yells and firing their arrows into the air when approaching a village of prospective hosts. The early trappers and mountain-men carried on the custom by whooping and shooting their guns in a harmless direction when nearing a camp with friendly intentions. The shouting was a most logical signal that he was arriving openly, while a freshly emptied single-shot weapon was about as good a peace sign as could be devised. When the cattlemen first began trailing their herds into what was then still Indian country, they followed the old practice of announcing their presence with gunshots when calling on their red neighbors in friendliness. Later cowboys simply perpetuated the ancient custom, often without knowing its significance. Anyway, it was a fine accompaniment to pounding hoofs and shrill yells; it lent a certain amount of excitement to the occasion, and it was a lot of fun.

Fun was the main thing. A cowboy would climb any obstacle to have a moment's fun. Unfortunately, the more-stolid townsman didn't care for the kind of fun that might occasionally disturb his eight hours' sleep or cause him to break the dignity of his stride to avoid the happily yipping centaur in fringed buckskin.

A not inconsiderable portion of this feeling was based on an unrecognized sense of fear. The workings of the cowboy mind was something entirely foreign to townspeople and men on foot. And like all of mankind before them when faced by the unknown, this unconscious fear drove them to take up arms in defense against imaginary dragons. As it was impossible to forcibly eliminate the lurking threat to quivering scalps and unarmored bosoms, they did the next best thing by appointing a quick-fingered gunman to dehorn it. The appointed marshal felt he had to make a showing in order to prove his worth, and the only material he had to work on was visiting cowboys. When some particularly salty individual objected to being summarily dehorned in public, the marshal promptly blew him apart in the interest of civilized progress and personal prestige. Then some of the cowboy's hotheaded friends—they were ever a clannish lot, and rather impulsive—set out to kill the marshal. That called for another marshal to square accounts with more cowboys. The first thing anybody knew they had the makings of a B-grade movie all laid out on Boot Hill.

But despite this apparent contention, most of the violent deaths in frontier cowtowns were not caused by cowboys. Then, as now, it was the marshals, outlaws, gamblers, professional gunfighters, and quick-buck artists around town who did most of the bloodletting. Of course, the cowboys also packed guns; and most of them were reasonably proficient in their use. Guns were a highly important part of their outfits. But their purpose was not to kill people.

Cowboys, as a whole, were as averse to taking human life as was any other normal-minded citizen. They did, however, need and use guns in line with their work. A cow or horse might become sick or crippled out on the range, where only a merciful bullet could end its suffering. Predatory varmints always lurked around a herd, hoping to pick up a calf or colt or pull down one of the weaker grown animals. Hydrophobia outbreaks among coyotes, skunks, and the like might create the demand for a ready weapon on any day's ride in any region. Guns were used for killing rattlesnakes, to turn the leaders of a stampeding herd, as a signal to distant companions, to bring help in time of distress, or any one of a dozen other most sensible purposes. More than one man, accidentally set afoot on the range among dangerously wild cattle, has had a few harmless discharges from a handy gun to thank for a safe return to camp. A suddenly spooked bronc might occasionally catch its rider napping and spill him out of the saddle. There have been cases of such misadventures catching the man's foot in the stirrup, when only an instantaneous shot from the holstered gun at his hip prevented his being kicked or dragged to death. Even on the curtailed range of modern times, a gun on the person of a cowboy who knows how and when to use it is one of the best aids yet devised to safe and sane management of his affairs.

Authorities tell us there was no one killed in wild and woolly Abilene, Kansas, until after the town installed its first peace officer. That was late in 1870, when the city fathers began conjuring up visions of more untamed barbarians headed north with longhorn trail herds. What such uninhibited wild men *might* do when they arrived was enough to call out all hands to build a new jail. The marshal was happy to bolster his reputation by enforcing the newborn law—until the happiness was transferred to a swifter gunhand. From then on, it was a case of trouble always being ready to tangle with suspicion. The larger the town grew, the more room there was for both trouble and suspicion. Boot Hill remained neutral and thrived accordingly.

The name Boot Hill, incidentally, was first applied to the cemetery at Dodge City, Kansas, when that queen of the cowtowns was established to give aid and comfort to Fort Dodge in 1872. The famous hill on the northwest edge of town was selected as a place of retirement for obstreperous railroad builders, hide hunters, and the riffraff that followed the rails west in hopes of salvaging the fruits of somebody else's toil. The cowboys who came up the trail in ensuing years, along with assorted gunslingers yearning for practice, helped boost its population and popularize the name.

Dodge City's originality is also credited with being responsible for a few other appellations still used in certain quarters. It was there that dead men, found stretched out stiff and cold on the street before breakfast, first became known as "stiffs." The customary aroma carried by some hide hunters gave rise to the well-known word "stinker," at about the same time. "Joints," as a term for saloons, brothels, and the like seems to have made its original appearance in the Dodge City *Times*.

Even that time-hallowed institution known as the "red-light district" derived its name from an establishment that graced the south side of the railroad tracks in Dodge. The madam of the palace sought to draw trade away from her competitors by furnishing her house in a very extravagant style. One of her more striking embellishments was a frame of red-glass window panes set in the front of the building. The place soon became known throughout the territory as the Red Light House. Familiarity and refined allusion to sin being what they are, the designation has come down to us as an everyday colloquialism.

It naturally goes without saying that some cowboys found well-merited lodgings either in the jail or on Boot Hill. They weren't all knights in shining armor, by any means. Cowcountry had its share of the ignorant and degraded, the mean, brutal, crooked, and vicious much as might be found smirching the ranks of lawyers, doctors, bankers, and shopkeepers. But such individuals never represented the true working cowboy any more than did the rotten apples in other professions. Neither did this type last with any outfit. Ordinarily, they settled like silt into the backwash of short-card dealing, outlawry, and hired gunfighting. A man had to measure up four-square to get anywhere as a cowboy.

The ranks of ranchmen can likewise claim no unblemished record of pristine purity. There, as in any society, greed, iniquity, and twisted minds left an occasional slimy trail across the face of decency. Power hunger or money greed led a scattering of cowmen to murder settlers, rape the holdings of smaller neighbors, corrupt judges and jurors, and pirate the public domain for selfish profit. Such infamies as men of this type perpetrated in Custer County, Nebraska, Johnson County, Wyoming, and Lincoln County, New Mexico, will forever leave their black smears on the history of American cattledom. They were as bad as some of the outrages committed by divers lumber barons, railroad magnates, and industrial kings.

As a matter of fact, the outfits which created the worst depredations and caused the most stink on western ranges were owned and directed by eastern capitalists. Many individuals or companies of this type used any underhanded means to appropriate the vast sections of public land which only their wealth permitted them to stock and to hold. The men they employed to do their dirty work were for the most part hired gunmen and professional killers. They had about as much relation to regular cowboys as New York's hoodlums have to respectable businessmen.

Most of the native western ranchers were ordinary, hardworking men blessed with a generous amount of human decency. The majority had come up the hard way and respected the rights of others who had done the same. Moreover, few of them had any great urge to rule a kingdom, while fewer still possessed the capital or political affiliations necessary for excessive range grabbing. Although often inclined to hold tough with what they had carved out of the wilderness, not many had the acquisitiveness that led to villainy and foul play.

Even the big furor over cattlemen going on the warpath against the homesteaders was far less the fault of ranch owners than that of government planners, railroad officials, and misdirected thinking on the part of the public. True, cattlemen were raising private beef on public land. And they were in active opposition to homesteaders bent on turning the ocean of grass into a grab-bag of dirt farms. Yet it must be remembered that it was the men on horseback who first settled the country; who took all the big risks in taming a raw, savage land so that men on foot might dare to move about with their plows and hoes and chicken coops. Consideration should also be given to the fact that the pioneer stockmen had been crisscrossing the western ranges for years, their discerning eyes ever alert to the characteristics and potentialities of any place visited. They knew what would happen in many sections if the grass should be turned over to expose the light and sandy soil to the everlasting wind. Familiarity with vegetation and climatic conditions had likewise taught them that many areas could never be crop farmed profitably; plowing would only ruin the grazing forever and give nothing in return. It was only natural that they should be opposed to foreseeable destruction. Had the authorities in government listened to their pleas that certain large areas of the Great Plains be set aside as a permanent range country, its ever-reproductive grasses would have provided one of the nation's greatest natural resources for all time. Their idea of an equable apportionment of grazing rights, with range fees in lieu of land taxes, was proved sound by national grazing programs half a century later. But at that time, single-track minds unable to see past the dust of an immigrant wagon had no ears for the minority who knew what it was talking about.

"Free land in the West!" was made to ring through the East like the trumpets of Joshua. Railroads promised a pot of honey under every sagebrush plant within reach of their ticket offices. Outfitters and land promoters gathered like vultures at the feast. No wonder the men on horseback viewed with hostility the locust-like descent on the greatest grazing land ever created, the destruction of all they had built by years of sheer courage and privation.

Much ado has likewise been made about overgrazing and wasteful erosion caused by the stockmen's greed. But here again, most of the blame must go to lack of agricultural foresight by men buried under their own shadows. The early cattleman took into consideration the scantier grass of the dry hills. He grazed them in the proper season without harm to the grassroots, reserving the more heavily sodded strong lands for later feed. Each year saw the process repeated without detriment to the soil. Then came the nester, under government sponsorship, to plow up all the best land. This forced the cowman to depend entirely on the thin-soiled hills, where steady grazing eventually decimated the natural cover, as he had predicted. The result was that the national policy killed the goose that laid the golden egg, the homesteader starved to death trying to eat it, and the man on horseback got the blame for everything from everybody.

Similar shortsighted, overall condemnations of unknown situations, shouted from afar by vociferous ivory-tower dwellers looking down their long, blue noses, were applied to the ladies gracing the frontier dance halls and less-reputable buildings across the railroad tracks.

Without wishing to spoil the pleasure of back-fence gossip and the rolling of outraged eyeballs, it must be said that a large share of the dance-hall girls were widows or needy women of good morals forced to earn a living in an era when dressmaking and teaching school were the only occupations granted the mantle of respectability for females. As there were few schools and less dressmaking in the raw frontier towns—and a dollar a day didn't go very far toward the support of oneself and perhaps a family, anyway—some of the more-enterprising ladies went to work at the dance halls. The majority of these were strictly entertainers; nothing else. The proprieties were carefully observed; anyone who treated them otherwise usually found himself in trouble. Their job was to sing, dance, and brighten the evenings for lonely men starved for a bit of feminine companionship. Their only sin, if sin it could be called, was inducing the patrons of the place to buy as many drinks and dances as possible, thus increasing their own revenue through percentages received on all such purchases. They themselves commonly drank cold tea or colored water, preserved a ladylike decorum, and went home alone to a well-deserved rest when the night's work was finished, much as do their equally worthy counterparts of today.

While the majority of the less virtuous fair ones living on the wrong side of the tracks fell far short of being the glamorous young beauties some television producers would have us believe, not all were deliberately larcenous, unscrupulous, debauched, offensive to the eye, or without principles. Of course, there were plenty of the unsavory type, as in any social circle, but examples of nobility of character were no novelty. Many had the looks, pride, and deportment of good breeding. Some had the frank unselfishness of heart which responded to any human need among their associates. Cowcountry annals are replete with records of such girls who loaned money and encouragement to unfortunate friends and acquaintances; who used their places of business as clearing houses for employment and the jobless; who gave their time unstintingly in the cause of individual distress or community need. Many of them, particularly in the early days, found love and marriage in the course of association, going on to become exemplary wives and mothers, richer, perhaps, than their more-sheltered sisters in the experience which makes for human understanding.

Dora Hand of Dodge City was as lovely and talented as she was kindly, generous, and energetic. Tales are legion of the unfortunates she grubstaked, the cowboys she helped out of tough spots, the sick she nursed, all without asking for security of any kind. Few people in Dodge were more respected. One of her old-time acquaintances, mentioned by Stuart Lake, voiced the opinion that the only low thing about her was her nighttime profession. "And I reckon," he added, "she even done considerable to elevate that."

Rowdy Kate Lowe, a prominent figure in both Kansas and Texas, left behind her an imposing record of charitable deeds, including the church work that profited by a goodly share of her money.

Inhabitants of the Idaho gold camps remembered Molly b'Damn as being honest, generous, refined, cultured, strikingly beautiful, and possessing a most attractive personality. Even more widely known were her acts of kindness, sympathy, and financial assistance in times of need. A widespread siege of illness in camp one winter found her promptly closing down her business while she nursed the sick without discrimination, often wading through thigh-deep snow to carry food or necessary attention to some invalided miner unable to fend for himself.

Foremost among the many humanities credited to Galway Nell of Montana was the hundred-mile ride she made between breakfast of one day and daylight the next morning. The journey was over a snow-choked mountain trail in mid-January weather. Word had reached town of a homesteader's wife and child down with pneumonia in their isolated cabin. Nell didn't even know the family; they were nothing to her. But the husband was away earning another grubstake, the woman had to have immediate help, and no one else seemed inclined to offer their services. Nell simply dealt herself in by gathering up a few necessities and appropriating the town marshal's big blue-roan gelding—then made a joke of the way her frostbitten feet shed three toenails the following spring.

Even that much-maligned frontier woman Calamity Jane abandoned her own interests the fall of 1878 to take care of the smallpox victims of Deadwood, South Dakota. When the epidemic suddenly struck that isolated town in full force, she promptly rigged up a pest house in Spruce Gulch, in back of the White Rocks, and proceeded to nurse the unfortunates through to recovery.

That this was no freakish deviation from true character is pretty well established by other kind acts credited to her. One in point was the time a man by the name of Warren was seriously stabbed in a fight at Deadwood the night of July 12, 1876. The fellow was in a bad way, and only Calamity was not too busy with respectable jobs to care for him. She trundled him up to her cabin and stayed with him until he was well on the road to recovery.

When a smallpox epidemic struck Kingston, New Mexico, the winter of 1882, it found the town with only one doctor and no one willing to volunteer for nursing. The doctor himself was in poor health induced by too many nights in the company of John Barleycorn. About all he was able to do was set up a tent for the victims and hire a couple of old rumhounds to take care of them. His medical assistance was a jug of whiskey left at the tent each morning. The pseudonurses gave most of their attention to the jug, while their patients wallowed in their misery and died unattended. The only thing that saved the day was that news of the growing debacle finally reached one of the red-light houses. There, upon hearing of the many deaths and the pitiful state of the living, three of the girls promptly packed up a few necessities and moved in on the pest-house tent. After summarily firing the drunken attendants and cleaning up the mess, they settled down to nurse the remaining patients through to complete recovery.

Whoever said Christians are often found beneath soiled garments was certainly not raised in an ivory tower.

Over in Virginia City, Nevada, we find another daughter of the oldest profession who refutes the undeserved defamations hurled at her class. Julia Bulette was tall, slender, and lovely to look at. Her nature was generous, impulsive, and rich with human kindness. She was never too preoccupied with her own affairs or the acquisition of money to lend a hand when someone was in need. She turned her house into a hospital and herself into a nurse when the town suffered a severe epidemic; she habitually straightened disordered rooms and cooked tasty meals for her friends; her hands never hesitated at sewing on a few buttons or mending a pair of socks for one of the boys forced to depend on his own efforts. No thought of repayment ever clouded any of her kindness. Virginia City, however, was not the kind of a town that forgets. Upon her death at the hands of a thieving hoodlum, the citizens, led by the volunteer fire department, gave her one of the most impressive funerals Nevada has ever known.

And these are only a few examples from the bright roster of girls who, among their less-admirable compatriots and the correctly unapproachable ladies from uptown, did so much to shape and perpetuate the finer instincts of the footloose cowboy drifting carelessly through the womanless fringes of an uncultured frontier. Most of them offered him rare moments of homelike feminine graciousness, a renewal of old memories and future dreams grown stale while clawing at the raw edges of a workaday world. Not a few met him on his own ground as active and enthusiastic members of the horseback fraternity, often going on to help build a dream into reality in some untainted valley that townsmen would never find.

An interesting sidelight on the understanding kind-heartedness often displayed by such cowtown girls and the standard of honesty common to old-time rangemen comes to us in the story of Cowboy Annie. Annie was a resident of Miles City, Montana. She had the misfortune to meet a certain cowboy, who shall be nameless here, when he reached Miles City with a trail herd at the end of a drive. The cowboy was one of those occasional unsavory characters who appear in range life as they do everywhere else. He professed to be temporarily broke while awaiting a forthcoming payday. Good-hearted Annie, knowing something of the long, arduous weeks on the trail, as well as the delays often attending delivery of and payment for trail herds, accepted his statements and extended her hospitality on trust. Unfortunately for her, later events proved she had placed her confidence in the one stinker of the outfit. After living with her for a week and running up a bill for seventy dollars, he rode off without paying her a cent.

Annie wasn't the crying kind, but word got around. When the

news reached the outfit, camped across the river, its foreman promptly fired the chiseling cowboy without ado. The other boys then took up a collection among themselves and paid Annie's bill. There was no thought of absolving the culprit, and they weren't overly interested in Annie's welfare; they simply considered it unthinkable that such a black mark should blot the reputation of their outfit, even though caused by a no-good misfit. Their company restored to what they considered a respectable standing, they saw to it that a full account of the affair followed the trail all the way back to Texas. There, the cold stares of men who valued integrity above all else soon cut the scoundrel down to size wherever he might appear.

Integrity was one of the truly great factors in the development of the West. It stood as a guiding light for most of the country's social and business affairs. Nowhere was it more in evidence than among the pioneer cattlemen and cowboys. There, a man's word was his bond. If his word wasn't good, no one wanted his signature. In that case, he might as well go live by himself among the gophers and rattlesnakes. And it was a hard country in which to get along by oneself. Thus it was that a mere handshake sealed most agreements.

Banks and banking were conspicuous by their absence in most sections during that period. Cash was the medium of exchange, with each man taking care of his own. Yet, robbery was seldom known away from the towns and stage routes. It was commonplace for individuals to pack large sums of gold and silver in their saddlebags on unattended journeys to and from market. Such men as Abel "Shanghai" Pierce took it as a matter of course that he should travel about the country with a couple of mule loads of gold coin, counting it out on a blanket on the prairie when he made his customary purchases of cattle. He, like the cowboy who left his latest wages in a coffee can on the shelf of an unlocked bunkhouse, or the rancher who rolled up his hard money in a buffalo robe at the head of his bed, gave no thought to possible theft while it was unguarded.

Houses and outbuildings were never locked. Friends and strangers alike were always welcome. If the owner was absent, they were privileged to make themselves at home, find something to eat and a place to bed down, feed their horses in the corral, and make any needful repairs to equipment at the blacksmith shop. The only requirement was that they wash their dirty dishes and leave a fresh supply of kindling behind the stove. In its decades of such practices, the old cowcountry experienced practically no abuse of such privileges. It was not until encroaching settlement and organized law arrived that the rangemen began investing in padlocks and eyeing strangers with suspicion.

In the trail-driving days, such long trips as those to the Yellowstone and upper Missouri River would impose a prohibitive cost on owners with small herds and little money. Ranchers of this type would usually throw their little bunches of stock in with some large herd bound for market, or entrust them to an independent operator who made a business of collecting enough odd stuff for a fairly profitable drive. In either case, there was seldom anything more than a verbal agreement between owner and driver. The former had only his faith in the other's integrity to ensure that he would receive full payment for his animals when the driver returned three months to two years later.

The same principles applied to run-of-the-mill debts, purchases made by neighbors on infrequent trips to town, and similar dealings. Old-time cowmen take a justifiable pride in the fine record of honesty that followed such practices from the Rio Grande to Milk River.

No less prideful are they of the average cowboys who represented individual outfits. Any one of the latter men might be expected to blow his wages overnight on poker and dance-hall girls; but, entrusted with a task, he could be counted on to carry through a couple of thousand miles of danger-infested country the entire proceeds of his employer's annual beef sale, perhaps risking his life a few times in the process. Although he was only an improvident, here-today-and-there-tomorrow drifter, without a home tie or responsibility the breadth of the land, any merchant would comply with his order for a new saddle or a pair of boots to be sent out to the ranch by some passing traveler without fear of not receiving payment the next time the man came to town. Ranchers thought nothing of leaving the work and accumulations of a lifetime in the hands of some devil-may-care cowboy who never had two bits ahead of any one payday in his life. The cowboy might head for the nearest place of pleasure the moment he was relieved, but, in the meantime, he would as cheerfully work twenty-four hours a day in seeing that no harm came to his trust.

This last characteristic exemplifies a tradition that exists to this day in any range country. No other businessman-producer on earth would think of scattering his investments out over a hundred miles of unguarded territory for six months at a time. Only a cattleman could rest easy on the reports brought in by his employees, or the critical work carried on by the same hired hands, without any particular thought of supervision. And no known class of workmen other than cowboys would voluntarily expend so much effort under adverse circumstances in protecting an employer's interests or giving their best for the good of the outfit against all comers.

Other traditions link the cowboy with the herdsmen of all ages. Concern for the animals under his charge rates second only to his respect for women. He would go on the warpath in behalf of either. Seldom will he look to his own comfort before caring for his mount. Money values lose all significance when he rides miles out of his way to rescue a ten-dollar calf—and probably carry it home on the pommel of his saddle. Personal welfare receives scant notice while riding out a stampede in storm-whipped darkness, tailing up an emaciated cow in below-zero weather, or trying to keep a desert-bound herd in motion until water is reached.

Colonel Charles Goodnight, who probably knew as much about cowboys as any man who ever lived, wrote that any real cowboy could be depended on to go to the length of his ability in doing whatever his job required. He said he never knew a coward, a quitter, a renegade, or one not basically square with his oufit to win any worthwhile recognition among the fraternity. Otherwise, they never lasted long enough to become real cowboys. Most of such misfits degenerated into worthless saddle bums, grubliners, tinhorn gamblers, or the subject material for fatuous writers of the more lurid Western dime novels. Genuine cowboys were the most misunderstood people on earth. It was the false misrepresentations of unsavory pretenders which so badly clouded the true characteristics of average rangemen.

The feudallike atmosphere of western ranches comes up from

the darkness of antiquity. Though not encumbered with anything resembling overlordship, servitude, bondage, or dictatorial domination, no other place so well reflects the medieval barony of ancient Europe. There is the chief of the manor and his womenfolk securely ensconced in the larger dwelling which commands the scene. Around it cluster the smaller homes and bunkhouses of his retainers; the shops, storehouses, sheds, granaries, barns, and enclosures for stock. Afield lies his principality, where his animals range and his fieldmen raise the crops for making his domain a practically self-sufficient unit. And everything pertaining to his holdings is emblazoned with a heraldic design in the form of a registered brand, his alone to flaunt before the world as proof of privileges bestowed upon him by the highest government authority.

In the old days, and still current over most of the West, a brand meant everything. Working cowboys ride horses belonging to their employer, thus identifying themselves to all observers as representatives of his outfit. A brand likewise serves to weld all members of a certain ranch into a closely knit unit, as solidly ranged against possible threat from abroad as were any knights who ever swore fealty to their liege lord. The brand on a cow's hide denotes her ownership no matter how far she may roam. A brand burned or painted on a chuckwagon or piece of equipment serves as a badge of introduction into any company.

By the same token, a cowboy drawing wages from a certain owner would go to war on behalf of anything wearing that man's brand. In pioneer times, this often meant riding into a gunbattle or traveling immense distances to recover strayed or stolen stock. In modern times, the same heritage makes the average cowboy a tough customer to run up against when anything threatens man, beast, or other possession of his outfit.

And it is his outfit, so far as he is concerned, in every sense of the word; as long as he works there, it is his home and his responsibility. Right or wrong, he will do his best to defend its security. Nor is this in any way the blind allegiance of servant to master. He would probably peel the hide off of anyone so careless as to confuse him with the servant class. And while he has all due respect for his boss, he definitely refuses to be bossed.

His boss, in turn, recognizes his ability to do whatever is required without supervision, treating him with equal respect—as man to man, rather than as employer to employee. True, the cowboy sleeps in the bunkhouse and avoids excessive familiarity with his chief; yet both eat at the same table, go to the same dances, enjoy the same jokes, and call each other by their first names. They will ride together and cook each other's meals while out on some range job. The boss may court the cowboy's favor in performing some extraneous task, while the cowboy may court the boss's daughter—if it's all right with the girl. The two may battle all afternoon over a two-bit game of horseshoes or half the night over a friendly poker session. To them, inalienable rights and the freedom of democracy are something more than a politician's catch phrase.

While we are this close to poker, it might not be amiss to pick up the back track of this traditional cowcountry pastime. Gaming with cards is as old as history itself. And nowhere has it been more in evidence than in the horseman's world.

Where poker itself actually originated is still pretty much of a conjecture. Devices for gambling were made by painting symbols on wood, bark, leather, animal skins, and the like as far back as prehistoric-man's activities are known. Every later civilization had some form of popular game utilizing objects fairly comparable to playing cards. A collection of Turkistan wall paintings from the 600 A.D. period display the familiar faces of kings, queens, and jacks found on modern cards. Perhaps further explorations into antiquity will someday link these and similar symbols found elsewhere with an original poker hand buried under the campsite of the world's original mounted herdsman.

Many historians claim that man's mementos carry allusions to the use of playing cards long before those invented in the Orient made their debut in 1120. The weight of belief marks their appearance shortly after the advent of papermaking, in A.D. 105. These creations were, of course, paper or cardboard of some kind, undoubtedly patterned after early forerunners of cruder materials. Their shape was probably a varied assortment of squares, triangles, oblongs, and round designs, as has been the case in later centuries. The type of games played are equally subject to guesswork, but it is to be presumed that they were of a fairly simple nature, something that might easily have developed into a rudimentary form of poker.

History tells us that Persia was playing an early version of poker in the 1100s. Some think it was their invention. More likely, it was an importation from the East or North, from whence came so many other things which these people incorporated into their culture during that era. At any rate, they had it. It was a game devised for four persons, using a deck of twenty cards. This was the game that the Arabs, Gypsies, returning crusaders, and Mediterranean traders carried as far west as Spain. From Spain, it spread north throughout Europe. The Germans called it *poque,* while it became *pochen* in France.

Tradition has it that the game reached America somewhere around 1800. The importation is credited to a couple of young men from Louisiana sent abroad to study in Paris. Whether or not the two viewed poker as a finishing course in education, they returned with enough poker education to introduce the game into New Orleans society. From there, it traveled swiftly up the Mississippi River to fan out west and east across the country.

This was still the old twenty-card game for four players, all cards dealt and the pot to the best hand—or best bluffer. It was not until 1830 that American ingenuity devised more leeway for speculative minds by increasing the deck to fifty-two cards. Even then, it was simply a game of bluff for the next thirty years. A person took his chance on what was dealt; there was no drawing. Ratings on called hands were: high card, one pair, two pairs, three of a kind, and four of a kind. Straights and flushes were not recognized.

Drawing to a hand was first introduced in the army camps at the start of the Civil War. Straights and then flushes were added during the year 1861, or early in 1862. Indices on the corners and printing the cards to display the same figures either end up came along shortly afterward, both by grace of American invention.

Following the war, the greatly improved game, so much favored by cowmen, cavalrymen, and riverboat gamblers, drifted west to the frontier. There, the cowboy taught it to the trapper and the Indian, who all accepted it as their own. Whether played with shiny new pasteboards in a plush gambling house or on a blanket on the prairie, using the crude rawhide cards made by Comanche or Apache, it soon won a universal position throughout the West. And it was there that it was improved to its present standards and the variations of stud invented.

*Chapter XIV*

RAWHIDE AND SADDLE LEATHER

To a good many confirmed disciples of gasoline and rubber tires, the horse stands as a first-class subject for rude jokes. The man who uses him with any show of appreciation and respect rates even higher in the field of low comedy. Mention of speed or efficiency in regard to either is sure to bring forth a six-cylinder belly laugh from the carbon circuit.

This old-fashioned pair is, fortunately, able to counter with a pretty good horse laugh of its own. Such rebuttals usually contain some rather pointed allusions to going places and doing things without the aid of three or four thousand dollars worth of mortgaged machinery, a bonded highway, and a pocketful of gasoline credit cards charged to next winter's income. They will probably also be extended to cover a generous portion of American landscape which is still not dedicated to six-inch clearances and a wad of additional taxpayers' money. And last, but not least, the uninformed will learn through long and emphatic, if not acidly profane, discourse that the man on horseback never had anything in common with the snail and the tortoise—or the motorist denied certain sculpturings of nature assessed against various unborn grandsons. If his ears or his patience does not fail him, the listener will likewise find each bit of information neatly wrapped up in a page of irrefutable horseback history.

Among the many proofs of equine efficiency so proudly flaunted in the face of machine-age skeptics will appear various notable feats recorded in the annals of the famed Pony Express of 1860–61. While this operation was a relay proposition, with a change of mounts scheduled for every ten or fifteen miles, the fact remains that conditions on the frontier at that time created unpredictable contingencies which often resulted in demands not encountered in any rule books. Even at its best, the task of maintaining a 250-mile daily average over 1,980 miles of roadless, Indian-infested wilderness was something to stir the imagination. But when critical emergencies arose in the wake of stolen horses, burned stations, and slain personnel, it was the wit, courage, and phenomenal hardihood of individual Pony boys that went on from where the book left off to establish an unbroken record of continuous service with only one mail lost in the 650,000 miles traveled during the line's eighteen months of existence. Examples of such single-handed performances are legion.

For instance, when the Paiutes were raiding all along the line in western Nevada, in 1860, Bob Haslam finished his seventy-five-mile ride from Friday Station to Buckland's to find all the horses gone and no rider to meet him. Pausing only to water his mount, he pushed on the sixty-five miles to Carson Sink and Sand Springs. There was no rider there, either, but he got a fresh horse. Another fifty miles brought him to Smith's Creek, where he met Jay Kelly. The two exchanged mails there, and Haslam returned immediately over the same route, completing his 380-mile ride in thirty-six hours.

Further Indian troubles in Wyoming forced a similar ride on Henry Avis the following spring. Avis finished his regular run from Mud Springs to Fort Laramie and Horseshoe Creek only to learn that his relief rider had failed to show up. Changing to a fresh mount, he went on to Deer Creek. There, he found that the station had been raided and all the horses stolen. He hurriedly retraced his steps back to Mud Springs, having been just sixteen hours in covering the 220 miles.

Wyoming was also the scene of William F. "Buffalo Bill" Cody's ride of 384 miles without rest in twenty-one hours and forty minutes. He had come the 116 miles from Red Buttes to find that his expected relief rider at Sweetwater Crossing had been killed in a fight the night before. Cody promptly took over the dead man's seventy-six-mile run to Rocky Ridge. Then, with no one to take his place there, he returned over the 192 miles to Red Buttes in one continuous ride.

Harry Roff made the fifty-five miles from Sacramento to Placerville in two hours and forty-five minutes. Another rider carried the notice of Lincoln's first election from St. Joe to Denver in sixty-nine hours. Jim Moore once made a 280-mile ride east from Julesburg in twenty-two hours.

Nor was all this riding conducted under favorable conditions. The mail had to go through without pause, regardless of hostile threats, prairie mud, mountain snows, blazing sun, swirling blizzards, bad trails, or no trails at all. Riders were in the saddle day and night. They often slept to the swaying of their mounts as they loped across the unpeopled wastes. Henry Worley and Richard King once met and passed each other in the darkness between Salt Lake City and Bear River, both sound asleep and neither seeing the other.

It was this same Richard King who once rode the 145 miles from Salt Lake City to Ham's Fork, Wyoming, in thirteen hours. A companion rider covered the last 75 miles of his route into Salt Lake City from the west in five and a quarter hours. He faced a driving rain all the way.

In considering the horses these men rode, one should not lose sight of the fact that they were mostly ordinary mustangs and saddle stock native to the West. Speed and endurance were the only requirements. The men themselves were of a similar breed, rawhide- and whang-leather cured on the western plains and designed to wear indefinitely.

It was such a man and such a horse that General Phil Sheridan was looking for when he selected Bill Cody to carry dispatches 355 miles to several Kansas forts in 1868. Cody stayed in the saddle fifty-eight hours to complete his mission.

From other old army records we find that it took Lieutenant Wood only twelve hours to lead a whole cavalry troop seventy miles in 1879. That same year, Captain Fountain covered eighty-four miles in eight hours on one notable occasion, while some couriers rode from Thornton's "Rat Hole" to General Merritt's Column for help, a distance of 170 miles, in something less than twenty-four hours. The 140 miles from Fort Harney to Fort Warner, half of it over sand, was ridden by four men of the 1st

Cavalry in eighteen and a half hours. A couple of dispatch bearers of the 8th Cavalry covered 110 miles in twenty hours in 1891.

All these riders were mounted on ordinary troop horses taken off the picket line and shoved through without remounts. The men all used regulation equipment. Their feats were considered little more than routine affairs in the service, and represent only a few examples of such accomplishments made necessary by frontier campaigning.

In his book, *A Senator of the Fifties,* Jeremiah Lynch tells of a ride made from Los Angeles to Monterey, California, by Colonel John Frémont and two companions in 1847. The three men left Los Angeles, driving six extra horses before them. They made 125 miles the first day, changing mounts every twenty miles. A like distance was covered the second day. The third day tallied eighty miles after 11 A.M. They reached Monterey the fourth day at 3 P.M., having traveled ninety miles. The return was started at 4 P.M. the following day, riding forty miles that afternoon. They covered 120 miles the next day, and 130 miles on each of the two succeeding days. Their actual riding time for the 840 miles was seventy-six hours. The entire route was over raw country and rough, wild trails.

Incidentally, Frémont's favorite mount, which he called Sacramento, was an iron-gray California mustang from the Tulare country, obtained from Captain John Sutter in 1844. Frémont rode him back to Missouri later that year. The animal was still under his saddle when he returned to California in 1845 as commander of a third western expedition. Sacramento was said to have had a nose equal to that of a bloodhound in scenting out enemies along the trail. Frémont claimed it was the best horse he ever rode.

It was during Frémont's occupation of California in 1846 that Lean John Brown rode five hundred miles in five days to bring help from San Francisco to Captain Gillespie's besieged forces at Los Angeles.

One of the most notable distance rides on a single horse was perhaps that of Sotnik Dmitri Peshkof during the winter of 1890–91. Peshkof's tough little cossack pony, Seri, carried him fifty-five hundred miles across the width of Siberia, from the Pacific Coast to St. Petersburg, in 195 days. His 149 days of actual traveling time, exclusive of layovers, averaged thirty-seven miles per day. Much of the distance was over Siberia's snow-blanketed plains.

In South America, in 1767, a fellow by the name of Merlo clipped off a three-thousand-mile ride in forty days. He was carrying orders from Buenos Aires to Lima, Peru, for Argentina's General Bucarelli. His route lay across the trackless pampas and leagues of waterless desert to be climaxed by the long, tortuous, sixteen-thousand-foot climb over the Andes. To average seventy-five miles per day through such inhospitable territory for that distance takes a lot of doing in any man's language.

As though to prove there was nothing phony about the deal, another individual made the same trip in 1806. The latter was one day longer in carrying to Lima the news of the capitulation of General Beresford's forces to the Argentine patriots.

In 1802, the adjutant of Argentine's General Belgrano delivered to Buenos Aires the news of an important victory, riding the 750 miles from Tucumán in six days. A decade later, Major Corvalan covered the 665 miles from Buenos Aires to Mendoza in five days.

It was in 1810 that one Guana, who had escaped from the vindictive governor of Salta, rode the 1,300 miles to Buenos Aires at the rate of 110 miles a day. A Lieutenant Samaniego fled from the Argentine defeat at Cancha Rayada in 1818, crossing the Andes to Santiago, Chili, with a total of twenty-seven hours for the 240 miles. A brother officer, who took off in the opposite direction, reached safety four days and 440 miles later.

Returning to the North, we find that Don Rafael Amador rode from Mexico City to San Francisco in forty days. This was in 1834. He was a dispatch rider carrying important government messages to the latter settlement.

Another type of distance riding took place within San Francisco itself in 1858. There, J. Powers rode 150 miles in six and three-quarter hours as an exhibition. Ten years later, N. H. Mowery rode 300 miles in fourteen hours and nine minutes on the San Francisco racetrack, to the delight of a large audience. Then, to follow the good old American custom, a Mr. Anderson soon came up with a performance that covered 1,304 miles in ninety hours on the same track. The fact that these men all used relays of mounts made it really more of a test of riders than of horses.

An actual race that may hold the record for distance on a single horse was the 1,800-mile run from Galveston, Texas, to Rutland, Vermont, in 1886. The prize for the winner was three thousand dollars in cash. There were fifty-six entries in the event. Each man had a single mount, which was to serve for the duration of the race, when they jogged out of Galveston on September 6. The contestants were limited to a ten-hour ride each day, the only important rule governing the race. Otherwise, it was every man to his own judgment. Evidently, there was some lack of judgment along the way. When Frank Hopkins rode into Rutland thirty-one days later, there was no one to contest his claim for the prize. Two others arrived two weeks later, the only ones to finish the race. The others gave it up as a bad job after Hopkins gained a long lead. They knew a stern chase was hopeless once they fell any great distance behind the eight-hundred-pound, seven-year-old, dun mustang stud Hopkins rode.

Over in New Mexico, also in 1886, a much shorter race for even higher stakes was run between Billy King, an Arizona cowboy, and a professional velocipede racer. The course was the fifty-mile stretch between Silver City and Deming. The match was the outcome of a bet of two thousand steers made between two sportive cattlemen. The fellow who backed the horse won the steers.

Another big bet, in 1848, sparked a race against time over the Santa Fe Trail. Francis Xavier Aubrey, a half-pint French-Canadian trader, had ridden the eight hundred miles from Santa Fe to Independence, Missouri, in twelve days during December of the preceding year. Back at Santa Fe in May 1848, he set out again for Independence, determined to better his own record. He made that trip in eight days and ten hours, including a forty-mile walk after some Indians stole his horse and outfit. Returning to Santa Fe late that summer, he posted a five-thousand-dollar bet that he could accomplish the ride in six days. His challenge was accepted and he left Santa Fe on September 12, carrying a copy of the Santa Fe *Republican* just off the press. Five days and sixteen hours later he rode into Independence, having eaten nothing, slept two and a half hours, ridden down six horses, and walked twenty miles. One two-hundred-mile section of the trip was covered in twenty-six hours of continuous riding on a single horse, a yellow mare he called Dolly.

Eight men took part in a race from Chadron, Nebraska, to Chicago, Illinois, in 1893. The prize was one thousand dollars. Each man had two horses when the eight started from Chadron at 5 A.M. on June 13. They ran into miserable rainy weather in eastern Nebraska, which continued to keep them slogging through deep mud most of the way across Iowa. The two top riders, John Berry and Joe Gillespie, battled for the lead across most of the latter state. Berry wore out one horse, which he had to leave at De Kalb, but he managed to win the race on his remaining mount. Gillespie, however, was right at his heels when they rode into Chicago the forenoon of June 17. And Gillespie still had both of his horses.

It was not a race for proffered prizes, but a race to save his own fortune that prompted Louis Remme to create a chapter of hoofbeat history in 1855. Remme was at Sacramento, California, on February 2 of that year when he received a draft on the Adams and Company Bank of San Francisco for twelve thousand dollars. Unfortunately, he delayed cashing the draft until the following morning. Meanwhile, the San Francisco bank had become a financial casualty overnight. This failure caused its branch banks, including the one in Sacramento, to close their doors immediately. Remme heard the news with dismay when he came down to breakfast the morning of the 3rd. The now-worthless draft represented all of his immediate future. And twelve thousand dollars was a lot of money.

But, and his thoughts were racing, there was still a chance. It was a slim possibility, but worth a try. His mind swiftly counted the odds against him. The San Francisco firm had a branch bank in Portland, Oregon, seven hundred miles away. The northern bank would not close until word reached there from San Francisco; and that word would have to go by sea, the only direct line of communication with the Columbia River region at that time. The ship which would unquestionably carry the fatal news, the *Columbia,* was scheduled to depart from San Francisco that morning. Its sailing time to Portland was six days. His one long chance was to beat the boat to Oregon and cash his draft before the Portland bank received the order to close its doors.

Remme wasted no time wondering if it could be done. Within minutes, he had a horse saddled and, with the precious draft in his pocket, was headed north. Trading or buying fresh mounts wherever he could, he reached the Oregon border at the end of the third day. The fifth day saw him pass through Eugene, and the following morning found him at French Prairie. It was 10:30 A.M. on the sixth day when he loped through Oregon City. A little over two hours later, he was braced wearily against the cashier's cage in the Portland bank when the *Columbia* whistled for a landing at the nearby wharf. A slow, satisfied grin cracked his dust-caked lips as he stuffed the last of the twelve thousand dollars into his pockets and turned toward the door.

In March 1859, Ben Snipes rode the 286 miles from The Dalles, Oregon, to Lake Oyosoos, British Columbia, in three days, ferrying the Columbia River once and swimming it twice en route. He rode down to the lake just sixty-two hours after leaving The Dalles. He had covered eighty-odd miles the first day, and around a hundred on each of the days following, resting during the nights while his roan gelding refurbished its strength on the winter-cured bunchgrass.

On another occasion, three years later, he rode a mule carrying fifty thousand dollars in gold dust the 600 miles from the Caribou country of British Columbia to the Columbia River shortly below Rock Island, Washington, in six days. Then, after a day's rest, he rode another 110 miles over the mountains via Colockum Pass to the vicinity of Yakima. Danger of robbery of his golden cargo forced him to make most of the journey in darkness, grazing and resting the mule in secluded coulees during the daytime. Neither he nor the animal suffered any ill effects from the experience.

Down in Texas, it was the birth of a new daughter that evoked a very notable ride. W. R. Messengale returned from a trail drive to the railroad in the shortening days of October 1870. Reaching Austin, he found a letter from his wife announcing the arrival of the child. It was a wish come true for Messengale, and he would brook no delay in viewing the realization. He left Austin shortly after sunup and reached the ranch, 110 miles distant, at 3 P.M. that afternoon.

Frank Stillwell did almost as well in March 1882, when he rode from Tombstone to Tucson, Arizona, the night Morgan Earp was shot. The distance between the two towns is around seventy miles as the crow flies. It was considerably farther by the winding, unimproved trail Stillwell was forced to follow through the mountains. He didn't leave Tombstone until after midnight, yet he had himself established as being in Tucson before daybreak.

Of a more leisurely nature was the ride made by Bill and Bert Gabriel of Sheridan, Wyoming, between June 5 and September 6, 1897. As sort of a stamina test for green mustangs, sponsored by Dr. William A. Bruett of the U. S. Bureau of Animal Industry, these men roped out two average green broncs fresh off the range, rode them a couple of times to take off the wire edge, and set out for Galena, Illinois. The animals weighed between 750 and 900 pounds, which was typical of most range horses. They were never shod or fed grain on the trip, being grazed through the whole distance. The twenty-four hundred miles were covered in ninety-one days of easy going. Both horses arrived in as good shape as when they left Wyoming.

While this affair was arranged to prove a point under a carefully conducted experiment, there was nothing very unusual about it. The western half of the continent was one great riding rink for three hundred years. Rawhide men and mustang horses wove a network of trails from border to border. When a person wanted to go anywhere, whether it was one mile or a thousand, he simply saddled up and took off. Distance was of little consideration; barring serious accident, he knew that wire-hard chunk of horseflesh between his legs would get him there.

It was one of these horses that Richard I. Dodge wrote of seeing in El Paso, Texas. The animal was, to all appearances, just another ordinary Spanish mustang. The colonel happened to need a horse at the moment, and was slightly put out when its owner received his forty-dollar offer with undisguised scorn. Dodge's feelings, however, changed to frank respect when he learned a few facts about the beast.

The mustang belonged to an express rider then carrying the mail between El Paso and Chihuahua, Mexico, a rider who was obviously as tough as his mount. His route ran all the way through hostile Apache country. The continued Indian threat forced the man to travel only at night, hiding out during the daytime. Yet he made regular trips once a week, covering the three-hundred-mile journey each time in three nights. The man had ridden this pony exclusively for six months at the time Dodge met him. He was still maintaining the same schedule when the colonel was later transferred to another post. How much longer he continued is uncertain, but it was for a considerable time. And during all that period he used a regular stocksaddle, which, with the necessary accouterments and weapons, would have forced the horse to carry over two hundred pounds.

Much the same kind and weight of equipment was common with all western riders during that period, for all purposes and at all times.

It was a similar load that the strawberry roan from the Spur ranch carried when Jess Pollard rode him one hundred miles between sunup and sundown across the Texas plains. The same applies to Jim Wright, another Texan, who covered four hundred miles in four and a half days.

There was nothing special about either the horse or equipment on which Enoch Fruit rode for help in 1854. Fruit was working for Isaac and Humanson, traders at Fort Boise, Idaho, when the Ward party of emigrants was massacred by Indians at that place on August 20. He immediately took it upon himself to arouse the garrison at The Dalles, four hundred miles away. Without rest and having to dodge war parties most of the way, he reached The Dalles in four days.

Even at that, Fruit was luckier than John "Portuguese" Phillips. He, at least, kept warm. Phillips made his ride amid a thirty-below, December blizzard. His was undoubtedly one of the coldest long rides in history. It took place the winter of 1866, when five thousand of Red Cloud's warring Sioux had Colonel Carrington's little force bottled up in Fort Phil Kearney, Wyoming. The Fetterman disaster had occurred the preceding day, with a loss of eighty-one men. Ammunition was running low and survival of the two hundred remaining members depended on someone getting through the Indian lines to secure help from Fort Laramie, 236 miles to the south.

Phillips volunteered to make the effort. He left the shelter of the post at midnight on December 22 in the teeth of a paralyzing blizzard. Dodging prowling hostiles most of the way, and with only a pocketful of hardtack for food, he staggered into the Officers' Christmas Ball at Fort Laramie one hour before midnight on the 24th. He was badly frozen and weak from exhaustion, and his horse died on the fort's parade ground, but they saved the doomed company at Fort Phil Kearney.

Fully as courageous, far more extended, and as desperate in part is the saga of the old Oregon country's most famous riding man. Far too little known is the story of W. W. Pearson and his work as a dispatch bearer for Governor Isaac Stevens' Indian Treaty Expedition of 1855. Popular history seems to have pretty well overlooked this gentle-spoken, smiling-faced gentleman with the wavy chestnut hair; yet his deeds stand as strong and durable as the tough, wiry body which bowed to no adversity in the pioneer Northwest.

The thirty-five-year-old Pearson was a top-hand rider, all 145 pounds of him. This, coupled with his experience as a Texas Ranger, scout, and express rider, made him the choice for courier service with the expedition. He joined the Stevens party at Olympia, Washington, in May 1855.

The outfit left immediately for the 265-mile ride to the big treaty council at Walla Walla. At the conclusion of the talks with the Indians on May 24, Pearson packed the governor's dispatches in his saddlebags and returned to the capital. At Olympia, he promptly headed east to rejoin the expedition, scheduled to meet with the Flatheads at Hell Gate (Missoula), Montana.

His pony's hoofs had clicked off 1,124 miles when he pulled into Hell Gate. As soon as the Flathead treaty was consummated there, he started for Olympia with more dispatches. He enjoyed a brief rest while his horses were being reshod at the capital, which he reached on July 18. He commonly led a remount on long trips.

Pearson's orders were to rejoin Stevens at Fort Benton, Montana. This journey piled up an additional 1,450 miles since leaving Hell Gate. The last 250 of these, from Fort Owen to Fort Benton, were covered in three days, without changing horses or eating anything except a couple of grouse shot along the trail.

Delays in the Fort Benton council fortunately allowed the man to rest up for about a day before starting the 845-mile ride back to Olympia with the latest dispatches. Then, shortly after crossing the divide, he learned that the western tribes were all busy digging up the hatchet. His superb scouting skill was all that got him through without a fatal encounter.

The storm broke in earnest while he was in Olympia. The whole country was suddenly agog with news of the Columbia River Yakima-Cayuse uprising. The entire inland empire had become a hostile armed camp almost overnight.

The Stevens party had meanwhile moved on to the Teton River for their conference with the central Montana tribes. Pearson's schedule left little time for delay if he would meet the governor there. He also knew that the governor should be apprised of the critical situation at home as soon as possible. Despite all kinds of contrary advice and ominous warnings against such a suicidal attempt, he saddled a fresh horse and headed southeast from Olympia. He hoped to skirt the worst of the danger zone and reach an unobstructed trail through the still-friendly Nez Percé territory.

Luck rode his shoulders as he threaded his way through the raiding northern tribes. He reached The Dalles, Oregon, safely. There he swung east to McKay's ranch on the Umatilla River. He arrived there sometime in the night. Unfortunately, the place was deserted. The only occupants were a band of loose horses.

Pearson figured on a change of mounts at the ranch. With the household fled to safety and his own horse worn to a whisper, he could only help himself. In the first gray light of dawn he managed to rope a big, snake-headed gelding out of the herd.

The brute was as mean in spirit as he was in looks. Pearson had a tough battle just to get the saddle on him. He quickly decided he would have a worse job trying to stay in it. The horse was in full agreement with his thinking. It came unhinged the moment the blindfold was lifted. Bawling its savage hate, it started corkscrewing out across the flat. Pearson was riding with all he had when a bunch of scalp-hungry Indians broke over the ridge in whooping attack.

The barking guns and screaming warriors scared the buck completely out of the big outlaw, causing him to take off at a dead run. His size and vicious strength now stood him in good stead. Pearson managed to keep him headed on a more or less straight course, and finally outdistanced the Indians after an all-day race.

After dark, he doubled back, riding all night to cross the Walla Walla River several miles above the trail ford. Sometime in the early-morning hours he hit the camp of Red Wolf, a Nez Percé friend. There he traded for a fresh mount, which carried him on through to Lapwai, Idaho, that evening.

Some other friendly Nez Percé near Lapwai provided him with a fresh horse and a young Indian guide. Daylight found him headed up the Clearwater River over the old Lewis and Clark Trail. It began to look like success was his. Then, shortly before reaching the summit of the Bitterroots, they became engulfed in an early-fall, three-day blizzard.

Some three feet of snow faced them when they dug themselves out of their brush wickiup. All trails and horsefeed were buried under the frozen white blanket. Further riding was out of the question. Pearson sent the Indian guide back to the lower country with the horses. Alone, he constructed some makeshift snowshoes and went on afoot.

He stumbled into Fort Owen four days later, more dead than alive. However, he would consent to eat and rest only a few hours while a friend secured him a horse from a nearby Flathead village. Then he was pounding leather once more, down to Hell Gate, then up the Blackfoot River and over the continental divide.

The members of Stevens' party spied the weaving figure approaching their camp on the Teton River three days later. They said it was the first time any of them had ever seen Pearson completely played out.

No one could deny that the man had every right to be worn out. With only a minimum of food and rest, he had covered some 1,025 miles since leaving Olympia. The exact distance is problematical. We have no way of knowing all the ramifications his trail was forced to take through the leagues of prowling danger.

Likewise, the individual distances and durations of his other rides are a matter of some uncertainty. Routes likely were varied to meet current conditions. And seldom did those old-timers bother to record precise miles and hours in what was considered only everyday work. Reasonable calculations based on the course of pioneer trails gives an overall total of approximately 4,445 miles for his summer's riding. It was more likely considerably more than this, rather than less. Figuring the time actually spent in the saddle over the whole period, he must have averaged in the neighborhood of 70 miles a day when on the trail.

*Chapter XV*

## NEW STRENGTH FOR OLD PILLARS

The old cowman was proud of his cowboys, his longhorns, and his mustangs. It was they who had lifted him out of the rut of mediocrity and enshrined his figure in the sun for all the world to admire. The cowboys could do anything that needed doing; the longhorns would fatten both themselves and their owner's purse, where the gentler eastern breeds would starve to death; the mustangs had no equals in carrying on the work necessary to an untamed, roadless land. The three together had built an enviable kingdom amid a virgin wilderness, bringing fortune and prestige from afar. No wonder they basked under the blessings of the old cowman.

The latter, however, was canny enough to see that the status quo could not be maintained indefinitely. He remembered what had happened to the Indian and the buffalo. He didn't aim to sit still while similar forces pushed him off the map. In fact, he had the route of his future course pretty well figured out long before any white-collared theorists got around to telling him how it should be done. Progress was on the move. The growing tide of western settlers was flowing out across the prairies like a horde of locusts. The only result would be the eventual curtailment of the open range. This would, in turn, mean a shortage of grazing that would demand less cattle of heavier weight and earlier maturity. The rapidly expanding railroads would also bring a need for improved beef to feed a burgeoning population. It was a future where rugged hardiness would be disclaimed in favor of more choice cuts in a carcass of greater weight on the hoof.

The ranchers of the Northwest, being primarily farmers and small stockmen, were first to hitch their black Spanish cattle from California to the wheels of progress. Long familiar with the beefier, farm-raised breeds of the East, the leggy native animals of the West appeared to them as sadly in need of being rebuilt. They lost no time in going to work on the subject.

This movement started almost immediately after the first emigrant parties began bringing their eastern cattle to the Pacific Coast. Although most of these animals were of mixed parentage, the majority could no doubt claim an ancestry dating back to the first recorded purebred English stock brought to America in 1783, by a Mr. Miller of Virginia, and Mr. Gough of Maryland. Later importations during the 1800s, however, helped augment the increase of high-grade animals throughout the East. The most notable of these later importations were the eight improved shorthorns brought from England in 1817 by Colonel Lewis Sanders of Kentucky, along with the thirty-one head Colonel Powell of Philadelphia, acquired to establish the first strictly purebred shorthorn herd in the 1822–31 period.

The year 1817 also saw Robert Patterson establishing the first purebred Devon herd near Baltimore. He started with a bull and six heifers. It was, in all likelihood, the descendants of those oirginal imports which went with the mixed herd of shorthorn and Devon cattle taken to Utah by a party of migrants thirty years later.

By the time settlers had preempted the Oregon country, the scattering of high-grade animals throughout the East had succeeded in developing a good grade of beef cattle in most of the farming sections of that area. As most of the westbound emigrants were rural dwellers, they naturally took their choicest animals with them as a nucleus for expansion in the Promised Land. They had reasoned well. Not only did their imported cattle flourish amid the mild climate and rich grazing of the western valleys, but mixed with the cheaper and plentiful local Spanish herds, they produced a markedly improved grade of beef after a couple of generations.

Starting in 1843, this development stepped up its pace soon

after small herds of purebred shorthorn-Durham breeding stock were brought to Oregon around 1848–50. Foremost in this advance were Uncle Johnny Wilson of Linn County, Sol King of Benton County, Captain Benser of the lower Columbia, and Territorial Governor John P. Gaines.

Down on the southern plains, the Texan was equally alive to what was going on. Despite his high regard for the old longhorns, there was no denying the preference for northwestern cattle shown by buyers busily stocking new ranches in the North. Also, the new packing plants in the East and Middle West were exhibiting a marked desire for the beefier animals. And above all else was the demonstrated fact that the heavier breeds could be brought to marketable age in half the time required by the longhorns.

It was early in 1876 that Captain W. S. Ikar of Henrietta, Texas, took a long, hard look at the future and decided that the third pillar of cattledom needed strengthening. In his perspective, the old pioneer West was running on a steadily shrinking rope. From eastern Texas to the Dakotas, a solid front of homesteaders was leapfrogging itself westward across the Great Plains. Farmers were cutting off the drive trails; new towns were spawning settlements on all the open grasslands; railroads were bringing swift and easy transportation to the frontier; fenced fields and pastures were beginning to appear along every front of the new order.

It was these fences that posed the greatest threat to the old freewheeling days. The new barbwire was appearing with increasing frequency throughout the country, barring trails and withholding select pasturage and waterholes for private use. Every new fence post helped foreshadow the approaching day when the raiser of four- and five-year-old steers would be shoved to the wall by men who could market the same amount of beef in half the time on half the pasture which unfenced grazing demanded. Yes, Captain Ikar decided, wise would be he who surrendered to the new regime and started his own fences before the neighbors left him sitting high and dry on a pint-sized feedlot.

The first invention of this menace to the cowman's old-time life, liberty, and pursuit of happiness on the open range is accredited to a Swiss iron-foundry man by the name of Grenninger, who was living at Austin, Texas, in 1856. In an effort to keep roaming livestock out of his orchard and melon patch, he enclosed the lot with a fence made by inserting sharp scraps of hoopiron between two strands of smooth wire before twisting the whole tightly together.

His scheme was a success, so far as preventing the encroachment of four-footed neighbors. Unfortunately, the two-footed owners raised such a hullabaloo about the lurking danger to man and beast, in such an unholy contrivance, that he was forced to do away with his creation. Grenninger was probably glad to have his display of European barbarism forgotten, without ever realizing he had given birth to a patentable idea before the world was ready to receive it.

It was to be another eleven years before the spirit of progress deposited a patent for a similar article in the lap of Alphonse Daff of New Jersey. It was perhaps some of the Daff wire that John W. (Bet-a-Million) Gates sold to a few customers around San Antonio in 1871. This, however, proved to be another unsuccessful venture. Daff's triangular metal barbs went down to defeat under the sharpened wire barbs patented by Joseph Glidden and Ellwood and Maish of De Kalb County, Illinois, in 1873–74.

Glidden fought Maish and Ellwood through several lawsuits over their respective patent rights. The only difference between the two patents was that Glidden wound his barbs around one wire before twisting, while the other company wound its barbs around the two previously twisted wires. Ellwood seems to have passed out of the picture at an early date, leaving Glidden and Maish as competitors, until the former eventually overcame his opponent to emerge as the nation's chief manufacturer, under the name of the Glidden Wire and Fence Company.

It was this Joseph Glidden who was destined to alter the entire face of the West, as well as the cowman's way of life, within two decades. And with him, as a salesman, we again find John W. Gates drumming up business for the improved wire, at twenty cents per pound. Growing sales, however, along with free enterprise, soon brought the price down to two cents per pound.

The new West was ready to fence itself in. Gainesville, Texas, bought its first roll of the new barbwire from the rival salesman, H. B. Sanborn, in 1875. Out at Amarillo, the same year, the Frying Pan Ranch strung up the first barbwire fence to appear in that section.

Another fifteen years saw the yearly output of barbwire mount from the 5 tons made in 1874 to 125,000 tons. The new era had thrown away the reins and was using the whip with both hands. No wonder Captain Ikar had joined various others in scratching his head for tomorrow's answers.

The first and most important part of the answer, he reasoned, was a better grade of cattle. As the kind of stock he envisioned was high in cost, as well as in scanty supply, he concluded that the best solution lay in breeding up a strain by crossing his longhorns with purebred sires. Unlike the legendary old-timer who was said to have selected his bulls by saving the calves that wouldn't make decent steers, Ikar held to the belief that he wouldn't have to worry about the quality of his steers if he had the proper kind of bulls to put with even the poorer cows. He therefore began to look around.

George Grant of Victoria, Kansas, had imported three Aberdeen-Angus bulls in 1873. They appeared to be first-class animals, but western rangemen had, for some reason, a general dislike for black cattle. A few Herefords had been brought to America prior to 1800, but their scanty output of milk won them the disfavor of most eastern farmers. In consequence, the breed had been rather let to wither on the vine, until Henry Clay introduced them into Kentucky in 1817. They met a better reception in the plantation South, where milk buckets and churns were not so highly thought of as an economic factor. By the early 1870s, various settlers had brought a scattering of these several breeds into eastern Texas. Although all were of good size and superior beef producers, most rangemen preferred the Herefords because of their ability to rustle a living under such adverse conditions as often prevailed on the arid plains and semidesert regions.

After assessing all the factors involved, Ikar followed his range friends in settling his choice on the Herefords. It was in the spring of 1876 that he imported twelve bulls for his Henrietta ranch. Unfortunately, there was one item he had overlooked: eastern cattle were not immune to the deadly Spanish fever. Only one of his new acquisitions survived to fulfill its mission.

But the captain was a stubborn man. And he still liked Herefords. He went ahead, shipping in replacements, until he finally established the breed as a going concern. Like the shorthorns of the Northwest, it required only a few generations of selective breeding to transform outsized horns and long legs into the more compact bodies coming steadily into demand.

Other cowmen, both South and North, had been busy studying their own crystal balls. There was no mistaking tomorrow's prophecy. Each year found more ranchers adopting the same program.

The north plains, which had formerly been courting the long-horn trail herds, were now casting covetous eyes on any breed of first-class beef stock. Purebred Hereford and shorthorn bulls were imported into Nebraska and Dakota in the early 1800s. Alexander Swan brought the first Herefords into southern Wyoming during the same period. Granville Stuart and Conrad Khors led the parade of Hereford and shorthorn imports that was to revolutionize the cowcountry of northern Montana. The late 1890s saw the metamorphosis complete. Although it was to be another thirty years before the West as a whole fully reached the ultimate in short-legged, blocky-bodied beef critters, a rosy twentieth-century dawn burst over the horizon to find a first-class grade of Hereford and shorthorn animals ranging from the Saskatchewan to the Rio Grande. Their longhorned predecessors had, in the meantime, faded into the twilight of a bygone era, noted chiefly for their rarity.

By the time advancing settlement had turned the drive trails into cornfields and barricaded itself behind a forest of barbwire, the cowman had his kingdom rebuilt in keeping with the times. In some cases, he moved to the mountainous territories, where national forest lands or untillable desert regions permitted a fair amount of free grazing. In many sections it was discovered that his early foresight and careful planning had won him extensive acreage of pasture lands, from whence his improved beef rolled to market in a quantity that rivaled the best days of the open range.

As the western cow found its way into the new day, so did the western cowhorse gravitate through a similar evolutionary process. Superb though he was in hardiness, durability, and skillful cow work, human egotism was ever eager to improve on nature's handiwork. Most mustangs were on the small side and inclined toward roughness. The majority were quite on a par with Indian ponies, a comparison decidedly unwelcome to many white men of the early days. Such individuals, usually recent arrivals from the East, harbored memories of the larger and more-graceful horses of the old homeland. They were aware that the finer-blooded eastern animals would be at a disadvantage under the rigorous conditions prevailing in the West, yet they couldn't still the longings for better-looking mounts. The only solution seemed to lie in crossbreeding for the better qualities possessed by both.

Along with this, the opening of the northern ranges brought a demand for larger and stronger horses, something more suitable to the deep snows of winter and rough mountain work in the Rockies. Too, the expansion of army posts throughout the frontier presented a growing market for mounts that would meet cavalry standards. The cavalry wanted the larger animals, preferably with an infusion of Thoroughbred or Arabian or some similar blood. The onrushing homesteaders were likewise looking for something better than undersized mustangs to pull their plows and wagons. So were the Middle West horse dealers, who had discovered the profit in buying cheap mustangs for resale as saddle animals and light-work stock among the farming groups. Thus, it was not long before the expanding market for higher-quality horses caught the attention of most western ranchmen. The resulting importation of pedigreed studs rapidly melted away the mustang hordes under the press of crossbred animals.

Of course, there were a lot of mustangs that escaped being promoted to the higher elevation. Although their extinction had been decreed back around 1890, they hung on in a somewhat scattered fashion until after World War I. They had many friends among the cowboy fraternity, who remained their staunch defenders through all those years. Many of them gravitated into the wild herds which roamed various sections of the West, until they were mass-slaughtered on the altar of gasoline and dog-food interests. Occasional specimens are still to be found in isolated sections. But, as a breed, they may be said to have crossed the Great Divide to join the mountain-man and the trail driver.

It was in the late 1880s that breeding for better horses began to claim the cowcountry's serious attention. Of course, there had been a limited number of individual first-quality horses in the

West ever since the American cowman staked out his first ranch. But it was not until after the War Between the States that they began to appear in any appreciable number. Several of the more affluent and foresighted Texans began working for improved horseflesh soon after their return from the war. The frontier army also brought a fair supply of pedigreed blood west in their mounts. Ben Snipes perhaps led the Northwest in this direction by importing purebred Hambletonians to upgrade his vast herds in the Yakima Valley of Washington, in 1864. Few north-plains and Rocky Mountain ranchers were without representative specimens of improved breeds by the mid-1890s. Preferred strains were as varied as the independent-natured men who owned them. Thoroughbreds, Arabians, American saddle horses, Tennessee Walkers, standard bred, Hambletonians, and others of less distinction offered a wide choice for all progressive breeders.

Most of them produced excellent cowhorses, when crossed with suitable mustang mares. Arabians won a goodly following in some sections. The sturdy little Morgan, almost forgotten except in a few New England localities, was turned into a first-class working cowhorse, to the great satisfaction of many. The eastern quarter horse was found to possess the proper build and sudden bursts of speed so essential to superior cutting-and-roping horses. The studied mixture of certain breeds developed the surefooted mountain climber, the swift-paced running walk for long-distance travel, the cutting horse, and various other special-purpose mounts. All were of better appearance, better suited to the outside horse market, and usually more adaptable to gentling hands than was the original mustang. At the same time, most of such crosses retained the basic spirit, stamina, and heritage of the wild, which ever characterized the Old West's unforgettable Spanish horses of the south plains.

Even the cowboy himself has undergone considerable change during the long march of events. True, he still does most of his work on the back of a horse. It's the only way range stock can be successfully managed in any cowcountry. He outfits himself the same as did his ancestors, speaks the same language, and moves with the same prideful bearing. He is in the main, however, better educated, more sophisticated, and enjoys a wider scope for thought and action than did his earlier counterpart; he sleeps more often in the bunkhouse than on the grass beside a bedground; his work, though hard and rough it may be, is more often interspersed with leisure; he wears better clothes, draws better wages, and seeks his pleasures at the wheel of an automobile instead of forking a horse. He may be a college graduate, well read, well cultured, and well traveled. Or we may find him to be a plain country boy, rich in the knowledge of his profession. In either case, he is a good hand, his background usually indistinguishable to outsiders and seldom flaunted as a status symbol among his fellows.

This, then, is the cowboy of today, standing as the end product of two hundred years of evolution, a truly representative citizen qualified to walk head-high in any society. Much of the roughness has been bred out of him through succeeding generations. The result is a finer-appearing individual better fitted to cope with the more confined aspects of the modern world.

Yet, like the cowhorse and the cow, nobody has ever been able to fully eradicate his basic nature. Underneath it all still flows that old streak of devil-may-care wildness, love of wide freedoms, irresistible independence, and pride in his heritage that has ever marked the stockman on horseback since the first barbarian herdsman rode down out of the Asian steppes into history. Thus we find him today as we have always found him, that indispensable pillar which, with those of the cowhorse and the cow, supports the cow-country in all times and all places throughout the world.

## Chapter XVI

## WHERE IS THE WEST?

Where is the West? People have been asking that question for three hundred years. When the Atlantic seaboard was first settled, the West was just over the mountains in Ohio and Kentucky. By the time the early colonists had killed off the game, burnt the forests, and seen their kin-folk brought across the sea to keep them company, the West had moved on to beyond the Mississippi. The Great Plains homesteader shoved it up against the Rocky Mountains, from whence it jumped over into the intermountain region beyond the continental divide.

Even today, the New Yorker and Marylander is prone to envision the West as being just over the hill. The Ohioan, in turn, sees it on the plains of Nebraska and Kansas; the plainsman thinks of it as somewhere west of Denver; the Denver man motions vaguely off toward the stretch of mountains ranging from Idaho to Arizona. Dwellers in Tucson, Reno, and Spokane just shrug resignedly and change the subject. But wherever he may go, the average traveler of today finds only a shrunken replica of the last place he saw farther east.

True, there was once a definite West, big and boundless and beautiful. It stretched from the Appalachian Mountains to the Pacific Ocean. Within its boundaries were held all of man's actual needs, free for the taking. Early arrivals found it a paradise, this bountiful West so unique from all other lands. They claimed it as their own forever, a fabled Utopia.

But they were not long content. Heedless of both the riches around them and the opportunity it offered to build a new world pattern on the dreams that had driven them forth from the old, they only pined for the things they had left behind in their former habitation, or longed for the new things an old regime was continually contriving to capture their attention.

With their minds turned steadfastly backward, they slaughtered game needlessly for the price of their hides, so that they might buy European and eastern clothes, furnish their homes in the old eastern style, and extend the structure of eastern customs throughout the land. The magnificent forests and lush grasslands were not like those back home, so they destroyed the forests and plowed up the grass to make way for the old familiar corn patches and wheat fields. The fruits of pioneer labor went to buy eastern materials for erecting ugly and drafty homes of eastern style. Hand-me-down eastern laws were cobbled up to fit strange growths peculiar to the West. Regimentation that had driven people out of both Europe and the seaboard colonies was revived as a cure for homesickness. And all the while, most of them used their spare time to build roads necessary for promoting a congested image of the London, Paris, Boston, or New York they had fled for wider horizons. Within the space of a single generation, they awoke to find themselves standing amid the same old frustrations outspread across the rubble of their brave, new world. The West that once stirred their imaginations to great heights had, as if in anger, slipped away in the night to separate itself from the transgressors by the waters of the Mississippi.

There it was that, in the 1820s, men tired of the cluttered East and, hungry for new freedoms, as their fathers had been before them, walked into the sunset with fresh hope in their hearts. This was the land of the beaver and the buffalo, where the sky was as big as all outdoors and a brand-new world stretched away into infinity. Riches swam by the thousands behind their dams in every stream. Here, the new breed of buckskinned rovers walked square into the middle of their golden dream. With no one to mark their course and no voice to govern their comings and goings, they found supreme contentment in the untrammeled wild lands. Life with the Indians was most comfortable and unexacting. The grazing herds ever furnished a convenient food supply. Companionship was plentiful, but they were not crowded. Indian maidens smiled appreciatively on the white man's attentions. Skins for clothing, robes for comfort, horses for transportation, and always the furry pelts to trade for any extraneous wants at the yearly rendezvous. This was the real West, their West, and they loved it. Nothing about it would they have changed or had come to an end.

Yet, as is ever the way with men, the thing they loved best was soon killed by their own hands on the altar of gain. Within two decades, heedless competition for the traders' wares and thoughtlessness of tomorrow had practically exterminated their chief means of livelihood, the buffalo and the paddle-tailed beaver. With this revenue gone, they took to guiding new settlers into the country and helping the army decimate their old Indian companions, so that still more settlers might come to populate the wild lands.

Thus it was that, by the late 1800s, we find the mountain-men living in their memories, still not quite sure how it all happened. All they could do was look sorrowfully back at the vanished West they had known and loved so well, and destroyed so ruthlessly.

It had been a fabulous era of bold, wide adventure; an epoch in which they lived the sagas that rang around the globe. Comparatively few men ever had the good fortune to see it as it was, or know the singular breed which gave it prominence before the world; no one would ever see either again, except as ghostly images outlined against the western horizon.

But it is hard to kill a legend. People of all lands believed that the West still lay out there somewhere; there dwelt romance, bold freedoms, and the fruits of shining dreams. When the cry of California gold and Oregon settlement began echoing back across the continent, the hearts of all restless spirits responded to the age-old urge of "Westward ho!" Their voices reverberated throughout the nation. The storied West would be their story from then on.

California, at that time, had created a culture that was beautiful in its simplicity and extravagant in its comfort. Colorful, leisurely, and the embodiment of gracious living, the great sprawling ranches lay in the sun through all the warm coastal valleys. Countless thousands of cattle and horses ranged at will from horizon to horizon. Time stood still while neighbors visited and feasted. Whole herds were often given to friends or youthful home-building aspirants. Carefree caballeros rode as fancy dictated, sure of a welcome at any *hacienda,* while soft-eyed *señoritas* lingered beneath vine-covered verandas to listen for the tuneful jingle of silver spurs on the flagged walk. Goodwill, peace, and full contentment moved hand in hand with the creaking ox-carts or tinkling accouterments of rodeo-bound vaqueros. Absence of competitive strife and selfish aloofness allowed free rein to the merriment around the barbecue pit. This was the West, a portion of the new and unspoiled world cradled in God's hand as a gift to those who would enjoy its bounties.

The newcomers from the East were eager to see it, to revel in its beauties. Here was proof of all the tales that had come over the mountains. To live the leisurely life of the dons, to rope the fierce grizzly bears and take part in the colorful rodeos, to ride the far-rolling hills and explore the craggy vastness of the mighty Sierras was surely the answer to dreams born in crowded cities and lonely little rock-ribbed farms. Here was the new, rich life they had come so far to find, the Golden West indeed!

But first, they must fill their bags with the gold that lined the creekbeds. The gold would guarantee full enjoyment of all this great land held. Gold was the answer to everything.

So they bunched up in a huddle of mean little cabins, such as most of them had fled from, and went after the gold en masse. Frenziedly, they dug and panned, fought and murdered, cheated and stole, with never a thought for the treasure that might have been theirs in building a beautiful and unique way of life so suitable to the singular advantages of this new West. Instead, they rose from the muddy sluice, their eyes so blinded with silt that they were unable to see the true solution to what they had been seeking.

First, they willfully destroyed the Californian's original western way of life and all possibility of perpetuating it. Then they began building tawdry imitations of the East on the ruins they had created. Gold-warped imagination was unable to visualize anything different from what they had previously known. The result found them ensconced in eastern buildings jammed into eastern-style clusters and filled with eastern furnishings. Eastern clothing and customs were sought after; square-pegged eastern laws and regulations were hauled overland to be forced into the West's round holes; more and more eastern men and women were encouraged to come and help swell the easternlike multitude which was swiftly strangling the true West on the gallows of eastern conventionalism. Overpowered by numbers, the West soon succumbed to a self-glorified homesickness for what they had sought to escape, masquerading it under the name of progress. The East had recovered her wandering sons. It immediately set them at work fabricating straitjackets for themselves in the old time-honored manner.

It was much the same in the Oregon country, throughout all the lush valleys of western Washington and Oregon. There, the early arrivals, fleeing want, oppression, and overcrowding east of the Mississippi, had caught the vision of the golden West and trudged across the continent to find their Utopia. It looked, for a while, as though they had come to the right place. Grass stood above the backs of grazing cattle; the rich soil produced fabulously; the warm, moist climate absolved the old fears of droughts, tornadoes, and freezing cold. Irrigation and frostproof housing were unnecessary. Encouragement for the erection of a western culture peculiar to the region lay on every hand.

Unfortunately, the seekers of new opportunities were unable to tear their minds away from old associations. With one accord, they promptly set about shaping themselves into the image of what they had been so eager to escape. They named their new settlements Aberdeen, Monticello, Sunnyside, and Davenport; Portland, Albany, Springfield, and Forest Grove. They built New England houses, Pennsylvania barns, and Illinois hostelries. Ready axes removed the forests so that they might feast their eyes on the homelike rocky hillsides, while expensive plows devoured the meadows in the interest of hoes and cultivators. The great cry was for eastern settlers, so they might cluster closer together and construct bigger and more congested cities on the old plan laid down by the East. And, as their homesick longings grew and expanded in the old homelike way, they emptied their garbage in the clear, sparkling streams to drive the teeming fish hordes out to sea and impregnated the water with the old homelike odors.

Again the West had vanished under the hobnailed tread of a

people beset by great dreams of a new world but unable to arise above their natural heritage. The wild game gave way to Indiana hogs and Michigan cows. Minnesota loggers stripped the evergreen hillsides so that men might dot their Iowa farms with Missouri frame buildings and line their streets with structures that might have been transported bodily from the poorer sections of Chicago, Cincinnati, or Pittsburgh. The great promise had been beyond the grasp of small minds chained to their ancient hearthstones. In consequence, another section of the fabled West disappeared from the eyes of man as it wafted skyward on the smoke of countless brushfires. In its place, a second-rate imitation of the East arose from the ashes.

Aside from the Spanish-Californian and the brief tenure of the mountain-man, the rangeland cowman was the only real Westerner we ever had. And his domain was the only region to keep its head above the swirling eastern tide and preserve a semblance of the real West.

This last factor was due to the cowman's stubborn independence, a pride in his ancient heritage that denied any foreign supremacy, and plain love of life in the spacious land he called his own. He alone, among all those with faces turned toward the sunset, envisioned a new empire of his own devising; not for him were the mediocre copies of old-world conception. He had found the boundless horizons and big, open sky to be an ideal setting for the western future his unfettered imagination pictured. That it might be a structure built in keeping with the country, something quite apart from the eastern farms and villages peopled by less-imaginative toilers living elbow to elbow, was something that only he could visualize. Slowly drifting his herds north and west, over trails recently vacated by the vanished buffalo, his thoughts dwelled on a West that could be made to assume, without perceptible change, an all-time stature such as no other nation could boast. It was a dream as broad as the country he lived in.

Those who saw and understood this symbol of man's ability to create a pattern original unto himself were a breed apart. They had little relation to the average American pioneer, settler, and colonizer. First and last, they were horsemen, rich in the centuries-old traditions of their clan. Bold in spirit and dauntless in action, most were spawned from that odd assortment of mountain-man, Indian, southern planter, midwestern hunter, American cavalryman, and Mexican vaquero. Tough, fearless, and imaginative, individualistic and self-sufficient to the extreme, each stood as a king under his own hat and bowed to no man. Their language was distinctive to itself, a blend of southern drawl and Rocky Mountain forcefulness leavened with liquid Spanish and all couched in terms strangely unlike those of any other American occupation. In dress, they were equally unique, their clothing and accouterments reflecting customs developed expressly for the peculiarities of their calling. Their work, play, hospitality, openhandedness, love of the wild, and carefree heedlessness were all utterly foreign to the rest of the nation. Few outsiders could successfully copy their visible characteristics; fewer still could understand the invisible ones.

It was this spirit, spreading across the plains, deserts, and mountain vastness, which established a culture diametrically opposite to the conventional-minded East. It was men of this type who gave the names Rawhide, Whisky Butte, Roundup, Buckskin, and Buffalo Hump to the scattered towns. They saw nothing wrong with calling a sulphur-tainted river the Stinking Water or a peaked-top butte the Squaw Tit. They gave such names as Hardware, Tequila, Smoky, Big Sioux, Warpaint, and Eagle to their horses. No less singular was the custom of a man going through the years under the name of Tex, Windy, Alkali, Buckshot, Two Guns, Badlands, or Skyline. Strangers likewise found themselves saddled with similar appellations appropriate to their mental, physical, or habitual characteristics.

In both thought and action the real Westerner stood apart from the rest of the country in varying degrees. He did all his work on horseback instead of on foot. He erected no fences or trespass signs to bar his passage across great distances, as was common among his more prosaic cousins in the East. His wide freedoms were little circumscribed by the host of petty laws with which a self-styled civilization felt it necessary to clothe itself. Anyone living within a week's ride was considered a neighbor, and none knew the crush of stifling multitudes.

The Westerner presented the first truly American architecture in his low-roofed adobe ranch house of the Southwest. The plains sod house and the ultracomfortable log structures of the mountain regions were equally in keeping with their surroundings and typical of the cowman's realm. That this cultural phase of the Old West was of worthy design is attested to by the belated recognition of such styles by former advocates of Dutch Colonial, English Baronial, and French Provincial types permeating the nation.

Everything was in tune as long as the old Westerner held sway. Towns were small and neighborly, built in typical western fashion to suit regional needs rather than imported simulations. Customs and costumes kept pace with the language and current activities so well adapted to the land of their birth. Business was conducted in its original western fashion, while the nation's beef fattened on a thousand hills and the cowboy rode his half-wild mustang into the hearts of millions.

It was a beautiful world, new and undamaged, set against a backdrop of great shining mountains. Nature was kind and the cowman's design promised a rich life for all of his followers. By and large, he aimed to keep it that way. And he put up a good fight to forward his intentions. But he had not reckoned with the overpowering odds against him.

Another thing that helped upset his plans was the fact that he was a very busy person. His efforts at welding the cowboy, the longhorn, and the mustang into a permanent support for his domain left him little time to watch what was going on in other directions.

Even if he had been watching, the insidious attack on his kingdom started so unobtrusively that it attracted almost no attention. It began when an imaginative Easterner drove his wagonload of goods toward the distant mountains. When the stranger decided to stop at the little isolated cowtown and set himself up as a merchant, no one saw anything but good in the conveniences he offered. In fact, they were glad to welcome some competition in the local trade. Furthermore, the newcomer was a charming fellow, full of amusing stories and pleasant manners.

What they didn't know was that he was also full of ideas contrary to their scheme of life. Almost the first thing he did was induce a band of his fellows to join him in a country overflowing with possibilities. Before the cowman eventually awoke to the ac-

tual trend of events, the strangers had joined in a move to re-
shape everything in sight along lines popular in the East. Their
forces already outnumbered the Westerners at the polls and in
policy making. Ensuing days found them strengthened by more of
their kind, along with the jackals which always follow the wolves.
And whatever each one's station or purpose in life, they were one
and all staunch supporters of eastern thought and methods. The
voice of the West was all but lost in the rising tide.

The golden West had ever excited the minds of men looking for
greater opportunities. Now that the cowman had helped the army
quiet the Indians and gone on to make most of the new territory
safe for boomers and tenderfeet, all those of lesser stature came
flocking in to reap what they could of the harvest. It was a vicious
circle: the faster they came, the faster the opportunities vanished.

First, they engulfed the towns, setting themselves up as everything from bankers and merchants to gamblers, real-estate promoters, and politicians. Most of them had no understanding of the
true nature of the country or its earlier inhabitants. As mankind
is ever prone to fear what it can't understand, these eastern-bred
footmen looked with considerable trepidation on the undisciplined
and carefree souls on horseback. Their one thought was to change
everything as quickly as possible, men and country alike, until it
resembled the mediocre level of the old hometown.

So they built a jail and hired a marshal to protect themselves
from the culture they were so busy promoting. This called for
lawyers to take care of the marshal's harvest; also, a doctor and
an undertaker for the ones who were beyond a lawyer's help. Before long, they were policing all activities into the mold of eastern
conventionality. The result, like the degradation of the Indian,
soon reduced the West to a land of shabby lawsuits, cheap politics,
enforced conformity, rusty tin cans, and flimsy board shacks.

Meanwhile, they tore down the old, comfortable western buildings to make way for second-rate frame structures modeled after
those so dear to their memories. They arrayed themselves with
all the habiliments of the East, while heaping ridicule on the
native minority who chose otherwise. The mores of eastern social
customs were fiercely promoted, as were imported sports, culture,
and entertainments. Anything distinctively western was treated

with the same spirit with which they persecuted witches a couple of hundred years earlier.

Then they persuaded the government to swap the railroad companies every other section of the cowman's grazing land for a rail line that would bring the entire East closer to their doorstep. The railroad, in turn, brought a new flood of pilgrims to turn the sod upside down and help shower scorn on anyone who rode a horse and disdained bib overalls, hoe handles, and milk buckets. In this, the farmer was gleefully joined by the townsman. The nagging envy both harbored against the unregimented, free-spirited cowboy, who was beyond their ability to understand, led to the frank hostility which was directed toward all the old Westerner's practices, customs, and form of speech.

By the close of the nineteenth century, the Old West that had stirred the blood of all adventuresome souls in all lands was virtually a thing of the past. In its place had risen a pale copy of the East. Each grubby little town was the counterpart of every other grubby little town along the line, all looking like vestpocket editions of similar grubby little towns east of the Mississippi. Townsmen and farmers exemplified the East in language, clothing, customs, morals, and business activities. Imported eastern crime brought more eastern laws, while the increase of eastern-type governing officials brought the necessary tax revenues up to eastern standards. Each new settler added another stone to the monument of eastern culture; each new contingent of earthbound footmen heaped fresh ridicule on any Westerner who would not forsake his heritage for a pair of stout brogans and a steady job in the cornfield or grocery store.

West of the Rockies, throughout the intermountain region of the Northwest, the transition moved even more swiftly. Much of this movement might be attributed to the peculiar characteristics of the Northwest's buckaroos. This branch of the cowboy brotherhood differed somewhat from that of his counterpart across the mountains. True, the buckaroo claimed much the same heritage— that of the Mexican vaquero and early mountain-man—but this had been tempered to some degree by an infusion emanating from the eastern-born migration which was so speedily abolishing the West from the Pacific Northwest's coastal valleys. Although he practiced all the arts of the cowcountry and envisioned his future through the cowman's eyes, his eastern-bred characteristics, so fiercely perpetuated by his West Coast ancestry, made the average buckaroo more easily adaptable to the creeping wave of earthbound conformity crowding in on him from every direction. By the late 1880s, the sheepmen and farmers had taken over most of his rangeland throughout the intermountain plateau of Oregon and Washington. Most of those who defied the hands of eastern reconstruction rode on over the Rockies with the big herds, and stayed there. The others came home and surrendered to the forces they were unable to halt.

It was they who met the westbound traveler on the final stage of his journey, still vainly looking for what was supposed to be the West. All the Northwesterners could do was nod vaguely toward Alaska or the Pacific Ocean—or perhaps Hollywood— the same as the Nebraska corn growers had pointed across the high prairies to the west, where the Colorado wheat farmers mouthed words about the Rocky Mountains and the mountain beet raisers waved off in the direction of the Northwest's prune orchards. From the Missouri to the Pacific, only neatly modeled replicas of the East stood as guardians over the grave of the West that had symbolized the epitome of romance for four hundred years.

Yet, the old Westerner was a tough customer. Although beaten down to a faint whisper by those who had come to enjoy his unique benefits, he still refused to wholly sacrifice his ancient heritage on the shiny altar of a factitious thing called progress. Hidden away in isolated mountain valleys or lonely stretches of untillable deserts, he, like the stubborn wild mustang or the gaunt gray wolf, shook his grizzled head and defied anyone to write his obsequies. In the end, many wise observers came to accept him at his own valuation, or even join him in recapturing the land he loved.

One great aid in this direction came from an unexpected source—the Easterner himself. The Old West had always been a magic lure drawing surfeited souls toward the setting sun, as had the sagas of the Westerner won an undying position in literature, motion pictures, and the artist's brush. Despite the transformation it had suffered at the hands of alien multitudes and mechanical progress, the West still cast its fabled image on the hearts of all men denied its charm. Surely all the Hollywood producers and

Western writers could not be wholly wrong. The storied lands must be out there somewhere beyond the wide Missouri. Minds thus turned reasoned that an earnest searcher could surely discover its retreat.

As if in answer to the wish, or perhaps arranged by the cowman's Good Medicine Worker, a few Wyoming ranchers conceived the idea of opening their homes to paying summer guests. This was in the early part of the twentieth century, when most of them had been washed up against the rocky shores of the wastelands by the tide of breaking plows and pineboard shacks. Visiting Easterners always seemed to have a weakness for anything pertaining to the Old West. Guided hunting parties had long been a favorite sport of those who could afford it while occasional sons of the East showed up at odd times, looking for romance and adventure. The cowmen decided that they could supply the latter factors during a few weeks of actual ranch experience, in return for the extra dollars needed to offset falling beef prices.

This decision met a surprising response. The West had something no other land could offer. Eastern vacationists made a discovery as great as had Coronado or Lewis and Clark. Here was a brand-new world, rich in all the traditional glamour that had stirred pulses around the globe. And the finest thing about it was that their visit included a personal touch with all the romance and storied activities of which legends are built. Horses to ride, branding to watch, dim trails to explore, chuckwagon meals, and ever daily association with the picturesque life of the cowboy to thrill the senses and feed the imagination. Here was something really worthwhile. The news spread. More vacationists appeared. The Old West was riding tall in the saddle again.

Along with this, reluctant ranchers suddenly began noticing that their dude-wrangling neighbors were beginning to spend their winters in Paris, Miami, and Honolulu, while they were busy scraping up the wherewithal to buy a new tractor or pay off the mortgage on the wheat crop. If cattle and dudes could bring in that kind of revenue, maybe they had been wrong in joining the alien rush to dig a grave for the West. As more and more of them returned to the ways of their fathers, and more and more dudes came to taste the flavor of the West, the general reversal exploded the length and breadth of the land.

The younger generation was, meanwhile, caught up in the flow of the movement. Cowboys, who had traded off their chaps and big Stetsons for store-boughten suits and tidy snap-brims, began rummaging in closets and barn lofts for outfits that would make them acceptable to starry-eyed visitors. Boys, once impressed by visions of white-collar jobs or hanging out lawyer shingles, decided to mend their ways after being shunted aside by contemporaries in Levi's and spurred boots, when glamorous girls from exotic regions hove in sight. Even the straw-hat-and-bib-overall gentry quit ridiculing the cowboy as they began appearing in curled-brim Stetsons and high-topped boots when they left the farm for an evening in town.

The townsmen were equally susceptible to changing conditions. The scent of profits emanating from visiting pockets soon aroused them to the need for old-time western trappings that had rescued the cowman from oblivion. The more-perceptive ones began restoring the old buildings and dressing their help in costumes reminiscent of the early West. Some of them even went so far as to reconstruct entire towns along their original lines, reaping fame and fortune in the process.

Others exemplified the program by turning their attention to the universally popular rodeo contests. Not everyone can afford a vacation on a western dude ranch, but they can breathe the flavor and excitement symbolic of the whole West for the price of a rodeo ticket in almost any arena throughout the United States or Canada. There they can, for the moment, feel as one with the legendary cowboy, the untamed mustang, and the equally wild range-bred cattle. A little imagination sets them back in time to the days of Colonel Goodnight, Oliver Loving, John Slaughter, Granville Stuart, Pete French, and John B. Kendrick. Casey Tibbs overshadows Babe Ruth, and they would skip an invitation to the King's Ball rather than miss the chance to shake hands with Dean Oliver, Jim Shoulders, or Walt Linderman.

Today, as yesterday, the Old West flames as bright as a desert sunset in the minds of most Americans. That is why rodeos have become second only to baseball as a spectator sport throughout the nation. That is why dude-ranch vacations charm the heart of an America that has never lost its vision of big, clear skies and wide, boundless freedoms. And that is why we victims of a jet-propelled civilization may still recapture our heritage in countless hidden valleys of the old cowcountry lying between the lift of the Great Plains and the western watershed of the Rocky Mountains.

As for the cowman himself, he is the same old optimist, still in the saddle and still ready to battle opposition to his way of life. His new rise to prominence and its accompanying financial returns have enabled him to increase his herds and expand his range over much of the area where his detractors once farmed themselves into starvation.

Although he may drive a new eight-cylinder job and mow his meadows with a tractor rig, you will probably find his saddled cowhorse grazing on the front lawn and a pair of spurs on the library table. His wife may read *Vogue* and *Holiday* and wear a Paris creation on certain occasions, but she can still whip up a hasty meal for a dozen hungry cowboys or heat irons at a branding fire if the outfit is shorthanded.

Their low, rambling ranch house, built for comfort and gracious living, has been copied from San Diego to Boston as a choice example of true American architecture. But for the cowboy's blue denim Levi's and short jackets, Stetsons and boots, most of the nation's vacationists would be at a loss for something to wear, while the younger generation would face an abject suffering such as they have never known. Western horseback riding has swept the country in a manner only equaled by the advertising business. The cowman's language has spread to the four corners of the continent, while his deeds occupy a generous share of our more-popular literature, motion pictures, musicals, and works of art. Some of his neighbors have even been chosen to sit in the White House in recent years. The whole thing boils down to a rise in western culture which has made the West as symbolic of the real America, in the eyes of the world, as has the cowboy become the symbol of the real American. Together, they represent the old dream of the early Westerner come true.

So the old cowman slides comfortably sidewise in his saddle to watch a new sun come up, while he rolls another cigarette. Life is pretty good, after all. He reckons he has had his share of ups and downs, the same as everybody else, but it seems he has made out pretty well in the long run. Meanwhile, he takes another squint at the three pillars he has been shaping up all the while, as supports for his kingdom. They still memorialize the indestructible cowboy, the mustang, and the cow, as they ever have. However, he now thinks he should maybe build them a little higher, just so nobody will have any more doubts about where he lives.

# ACKNOWLEDGMENTS

In building a picture that extends back over four hundred years, it becomes necessary to draw on material left us by earlier writers and artists whose contemporary views give us our only true perspective of bygone times. To all those whose works have supplied so many pertinent and often obscure details of the pioneer cowman's fabled West, without which this book would be sadly incomplete, I offer my most sincere thanks.

G. R. V.

Abbott, A. C. (Teddy Blue). *We Pointed Them North*. New York: Farrar & Rinehart, 1939.

Adams, Andy. *Log of a Cowboy*. Boston: Houghton Mifflin Co., 1903.

Bolton, Herbert E. *Coronado*. New York: Whittlesly House, 1949.

Bolton, Herbert E. *Rim of Christiandom*. New York: Macmillan Co., 1936.

Burns, Walter N. *Tombstone*. Garden City, N.Y.: Doubleday, Page, 1927.

Caughey, John W. *California*. New York: Prentice-Hall, 1933.

De Smet, P. J. *The Oregon Missions and Travel Over the Rocky Mountains in 1845–46*. Edited by Edward Dunnigan. New York, 1947.

De Voto, Bernard, ed. *The Journals of Lewis and Clark, 1804–06*. Cambridge, Mass.: Riverside Press, 1953.

Dobie, J. Frank. *The Longhorns*. Boston: Little, Brown & Co., 1941.

Dobie, J. Frank. *Mustangs and Cowhorses*. Edited by Boatright & Ranson. Austin, Tex.: Texas Folklore Society, 1940.

Dobie, J. Frank. *A Vaquero of the Brush Country*. Boston: Little Brown, 1943.

Foster-Harris, William. *Look of the Old West*. New York: Viking Press, 1955.

Garrison, Myrtle. *Romance & History of the California Ranchos*. San Francisco: Harr Wagner, 1935.

Haley, J. Evatts. *Charles Goodnight, Cowman and Plainsman*. Boston: Houghton Mifflin Co., 1936.

Howard, Joseph K. *Strange Empire*. New York: William Morrow & Co., 1952.

Hunter, Marvin, ed. *Trail Drivers of Texas*. Nashville: Cokesbury Press, 1925.

Irving, Washington. *Captain Bonneyville*. New York: G. P. Putnam, 1849.

Maloney, Alice B. *Fur Brigade to the Bonaventura*. San Francisco: California Historical Society, 1945.

Mora, Jo. *Californios*. Garden City, N.Y.: Doubleday & Co., 1949.

Mora, Jo. *Trail Dust and Saddle Leather*. New York: Charles Scribner's Sons, 1946.

Potter, Jack. *Cattle Trails of the Old West*. Clayton, N. Mex., 1935.

Powers, Laura B. *Old Monterey*. San Francisco: San Carlos Press, 1934.

Price, Con. *Trails I Rode*. Pasadena, Calif.: Trail's End Pub. Co., 1947.

Sheller, Roscoe. *Ben Snipes*. Portland, Oreg.: Binfords & Mort, 1958.

Thwaites, R. G., ed. *Early Western Travels*. Cleveland, Ohio: Arthur H. Clark Co., 1906.

Thwaites, R. G., ed. Franchere, Gabriel. *A Journal of a Voyage to the Northwest Coast of America in the Year 1811*. Edited by J. U. Huntington. Vol. 6.

Thwaites, R. G., ed. Maximilan, Prince of Wied. *Travels in the Interior of North America, 1832–34*. Vols. 22–24.

Thwaites, R. G., ed. Ross, Alexander. *The Fur Hunters*. Vol. 7.

Underhill, Reuben L. *From Cowhides to Golden Fleece*. Stanford University Press, 1946.

Vernam, Glenn R. *Man on Horseback*. New York: Harper & Row, 1964.

MAGAZINE ARTICLES

Ewers, John C. "The Indian Buffalo Hunter's Saddle." *Western Horseman*, Sept. 1949.

Haines, Francis. "The Northward Spread of Horses Among the Plains Indians." *American Anthropologist*, Vol. XL, 1938.

Kingston, C. S. "Introduction of Cattle into the Pacific Northwest." *Oregon Historical Quarterly*, July 1923.

Oliphant, James C. "Cattle Trails From the Pacific Northwest to Montana." *Agricultural History*, April 1933.

Vernam, Glenn R. "Northwest's Riding Man." *Western Horseman*, June 1956.

Vernam, Glenn R. "Packing the Saddle Gun." *Outdoor Life*, August 1933.

Vernam, Glenn R. "Rainbow Cattle." *True West*, August 1960.
Vernam, Glenn R. "Six Days to Fortune." *Westward*, June–July 1960.

NOTES FROM COMPANY FILES

Schnebly, Margaret. "History of the Bar Balloon Brand." Ellensburg, Washington, 1958.
Stetson, John B. Co. Philadelphia, Pa.
Strauss, Levi Co., San Francisco, Calif.

# INDEX